A Modern Guide to

Granny Squares

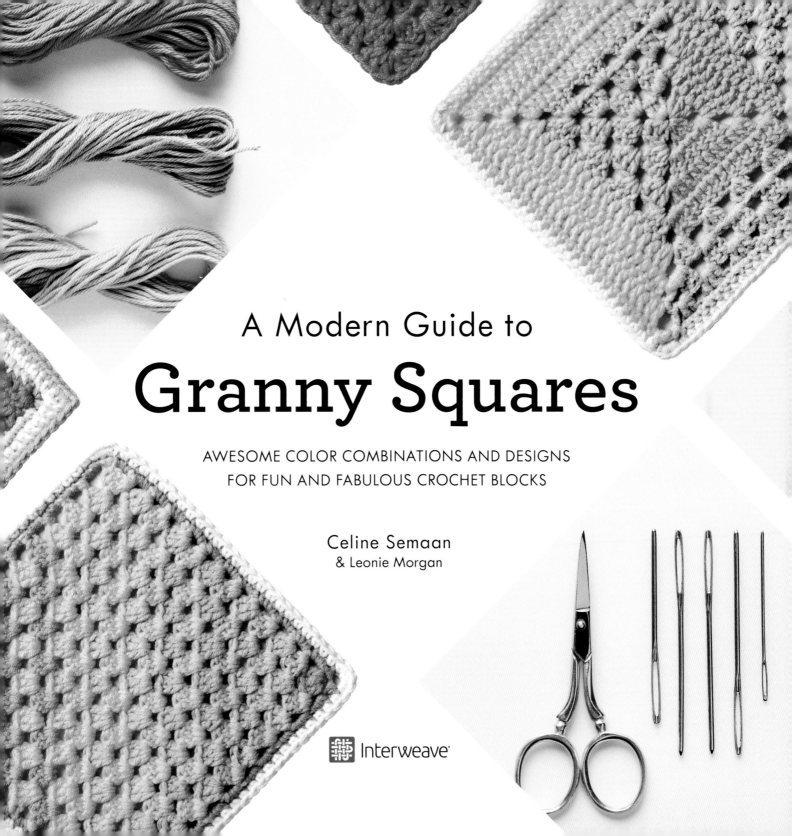

A Modern Guide to

Granny Squares

AWESOME COLOR COMBINATIONS AND DESIGNS
FOR FUN AND FABULOUS CROCHET BLOCKS

Celine Semaan
& Leonie Morgan

Interweave

A QUARTO BOOK

Interweave
An imprint of Penguin Random House LLC
penguinrandomhouse.com

Printed in Singapore

7 9 10 8 7 6 5 4 3 2 1

ISBN: 9780593332016

Conceived, edited, and designed by
Quarto Publishing
an imprint of The Quarto Group
The Old Brewery
6 Blundell Street
London N7 9BH
www.quarto.com

QUAR.343029

Copy editor: Ruth Patrick
Pattern checker: Linda Brown
Designer: Sally Bond
Art director: Rachel Cross
Photographer: Nicki Dowey
Illustrator: Kuo Kang Chen
Publisher: Lorraine Dickey

Contents

Meet Celine	6
How to use this book	8
THE GRANNY SQUARES	**10**
Picnic Time	12
Rainbow Popcorn	14
Sugar Flower	17
3D Heart	20
Pastel Grid	22
Citrus Slice	25
Bright Shimmer	28
Double Crochet Square	30
Intarsia Triangles	32
Modern Floral	34
Scattered Hearts	36
Single-color Granny Square	38
Two-color Intarsia Square	40

Colorblock Double Crochet Square	42	Cool-toned Triangle	78	**CROCHET BASICS**	**112**
60s Floral Motif	44	Dazzling Octagon	80	Materials and Notions	114
Houndstooth Pattern	46	Pop Flower	82	Starting and Finishing	116
Peaches and Cream	48	Crocheted Flower Net	84	Basic Stitches	118
Sorbet Square	50	Loop and Twist	86	Simple Stitch Variations	119
Diamond Daze	53	Watermelon Slice	89	Special Stitches	120
Rainbow Relief	56	Rainbow Arch	92	Colorwork	121
Sun and Clouds	58	Stripe Color Block	94	Reading Patterns and Charts	122
Jell-O and Ice Cream	60	Cute Kitten	96	Gauge and Blocking	123
Multicolored Target	62	Classic Patchwork	99	Joining and Edging	124
Acid Brights Flower	64				
Ombré Cross	66	**THE PROJECTS**	**102**	Index	126
Warm Tones	68	Rainbow Arch Wall Hanging	104	Credits	128
Technicolor Square	70	Citrus Slice Pillow	106		
Brighton Rock	72	Rainbow Chevron Blanket	108	+ Gatefold with Chart Symbols	
Four-leaf Flower	74	Minty Tones Storage Box	110		
Bobble Beads	76				

WELCOME!

Meet Celine

A classic granny square is the first thing I made when I learned how to crochet, and I have not stopped since. This book is an exploration of color, with countless hours, dozens of skeins of yarn, and a lot of imagination going into the bright and fun squares I have created.

For those who find it difficult to stick to one project at a time (raises hand), a granny square is just the perfect amount of crochet for one sitting, and reaching the end of a pattern fills me with a sense of accomplishment, as granny squares are like mini projects within themselves—that's what I love about them.

Within the book, you'll find a variety of squares—from your classic staples to over-the-top, unconventional stretches of the imagination. Some are designed to stand alone, others to be combined with each other, and with varying skill levels, color combinations, and stitch types, there's a square to suit everyone's taste.

By making a block at a time you can gradually build up enough blocks to make a unique project of your own—turn to pages 102–111 for some creative inspiration for things to make with your squares.

Crochet is a form of therapy for me. It's a fantastic way for me to destress and a way to express my creativity. Crocheting gives me focus and makes me happy. Oh, and the yarn…squishy goodness in all the colors of the rainbow.

Crafting should be an enjoyable experience and I hope the patterns in this book inspire you to play with color to create something that brings you joy.

Have fun!
Celine

How to use this book

This book is a resource of colorful granny square patterns that can be combined to create larger projects. You can use the blocks to make anything from blankets to bags; see pages 102–111 for four inspirational projects that will help you develop your ideas. At the end of the book you will find information on materials and crochet techniques.

THE GRANNY SQUARES, PAGES 10–101

At the heart of this book are the block designs, such as the sample pages on the right. With written patterns, charts, and clear photographs taking you through each design, you have all you need to get started.

Skill level gives a guide to difficulty: easy (one ball of yarn), intermediate (two balls of yarn), and advanced (three balls of yarn).

Block size is the finished size of a single square.

The techniques used in each pattern are listed here, along with a reference to the relevant page in the techniques section if you are unsure about something.

The colors and type of yarn needed to make the square are listed here.

The stitches you need to use to create each square are listed here. The techniques section on pages 112–125 explains these in more detail.

As a bonus, here you can see ideas for ways to mix and match granny square designs to inspire your creativity.

A key to the symbols used in the charts is provided on page 122, as well as the gatefold, which can be folded out while you work.

SKILL LEVEL

HOOK SIZE	BLOCK SIZE
US G/6 (4mm)	6 × 6in (15 × 15cm)

TECHNIQUES
Changing color on row/round (see page 121)
Working into round/row ends (see page 125)
Working over/into previous rounds/rows (see page 119)

YARN/COLORS
Sample uses Scheepjes Softfun

A = Light Rose (#2513)	F = Botanical (#2615)
B = Rose (#2514)	G = Cool Blue (#2603)
C = Cantaloupe (#2652)	H = Bright Turquoise (#2423)
D = Canary (#2518)	I = Orchid (#2657)
E = Mint (#2640)	J = Snow (#2412)

STITCHES
ch—chain
sl st—slip stitch
sc—single crochet
dc—double crochet
fptr—front post treble crochet

MIX AND MATCH

Page 42 ✛ Page 78

CHART KEY
For symbol key, see page 122

Using yarn
Round 1 (R
throughout,
ch 2 into ri
beginning c
Fasten off y
Round 2 (RS
[ch 3, 2 dc,
3 sts, (3 dc,
times, sl st in
(24 sts).

A written pattern takes you through the
pattern round by round or row by row.

Clear charts are provided for each
pattern with corresponding yarn colors.

Pastel Grid

k for trying out ombré effects.

ing.   Fasten off **yarn B**.

[3 dc,   Row 3 (RS): using **yarn C**, in any 2-ch sp, [ch 3,

hird ch of   2 dc] in same sp, skip next 3 sts, 1 dc in st sp,

          1 fptr around round 1 dc directly below,

          1 dc in same st sp, skip next 3 sts, [3 dc, ch 2,

2-ch sp,   3 dc] in 2-ch sp, skip next 3 sts, 1 dc in st sp,

[skip next   1fptr around round 1 dc directly below, 1 dc

sp] three   in same st sp, skip next 3 sts, 3 dc in 2-ch sp,

ch 3   turn (18 sts).

          Row 4 (WS): ch 3, skip next 2 sts, [3 dc in st

          sp, skip next 3 sts] twice, [3 dc, ch 2, 3 dc] in

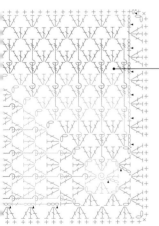

THE GRANNY SQUARES   23

THE
GRANNY
SQUARES

Welcome to the colorful world of the
patterns, where fluffy clouds float next
to 3D flowers and rainbows abound.

HOOK SIZE	BLOCK SIZE
US C/2 (3mm)	6 x 6in (15 x 15cm)

TECHNIQUES

Working with multiple colors at the same time/ tapestry crochet (see page 121)

Changing color on row/round (see page 121)

YARN/COLORS

Sample uses Scheepjes Softfun

A = Magenta (#2654)

B = Snow (#2412)

C = Light Rose (#2513)

STITCHES

ch—chain

sl st—slip stitch

dc—double crochet

MIX AND MATCH

Page 36 ✛ Page 38

CHART KEY

For symbol key, see page 122

Picnic Time

Classic gingham that would be perfect as a picnic blanket.

Using **yarn A**, start with a magic ring.

Round 1 (RS): ch 5 (counts as 1 dc, ch 2), [4 dc, ch 2 into ring] three times, 3 dc into ring, sl st in third ch of beginning ch 5 (16 sts). Fasten off **yarn A**.

Round 2 (RS): using **yarn B**, in any 2-ch sp, ch 3 (counts as 1 dc throughout), [1 dc, ch 2, 2 dc] in same sp; using **yarn C**, 1 dc in each of next 4 sts; [using **yarn B**, (2 dc, ch 2, 2 dc) in 2-ch sp; using **yarn C**, 1 dc in each of next 4 sts] three times; using **yarn B**, sl st in third ch of beginning ch 3 (32 sts).

Do not fasten off.

Round 3 (RS): using **yarn B**, sl st in next st, sl st in next 2-ch sp, ch 3, [1 dc, ch 2, 2 dc] in same sp; [using **yarn B**, 1 dc in each of next 2 sts; using **yarn C**, 1 dc in each of next 4 sts; using **yarn B**, 1 dc in each of next 2 sts, (2 dc, ch 2, 2 dc) in 2-ch sp] four times, omit [2 dc, ch 2, 2 dc] on last rep, sl st in third ch of beginning ch 3 (48 sts).

Fasten off **yarn B**.

Round 4 (RS): using **yarn A**, in 2-ch sp, ch 3, [1 dc, ch 2, 2 dc] in same sp; [using **yarn C**,

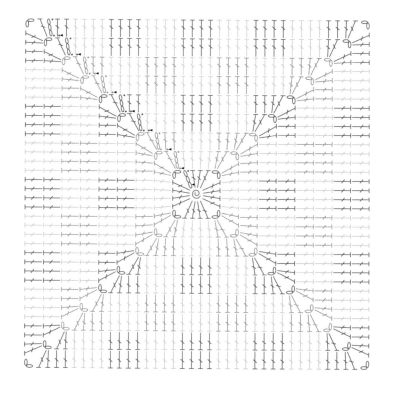

1 dc in each of next 4 sts; using **yarn A**, 1 dc in each of next 4 sts; using **yarn C**, 1 dc in each of next 4 sts; using **yarn A**, (2 dc, ch 2, 2 dc) in 2-ch sp] four times, omit [2 dc, ch 2, 2 dc] on last rep; using **yarn A**, sl st in third ch of beginning ch 3 (64 sts).

Do not fasten off.

Round 5 (RS): using **yarn A**, sl st in next st, sl st in next 2-ch sp, ch 3, [1 dc, ch 2, 2 dc] in same sp; [using **yarn A**, 1 dc in each of next 2 sts; using **yarn C**, 1 dc in each of next 4 sts; using **yarn A**, 1 dc in each of next 4 sts; using **yarn C**, 1 dc in each of next 4 sts; using **yarn A**, 1 dc in each of next 2 sts, (2 dc, ch 2, 2 dc) in 2-ch sp] four times, omit [2 dc, ch 2, 2 dc] on last rep, sl st in third ch of beginning ch 3 (80 sts).

Fasten off **yarn A**.

Round 6 (RS): using **yarn B**, in 2-ch sp, ch 3, [1 dc, ch 2, 2 dc] in same sp; [using **yarn C**, 1 dc in each of next 4 sts; (using **yarn B**, 1 dc in each of next 4 sts; using **yarn C**, 1 dc in each of next 4 sts) twice; using **yarn B**, (2 dc, ch 2, 2 dc) in 2-ch sp] four times, omit [2 dc, ch 2, 2 dc] on last rep; using **yarn B**, sl st in third ch of beginning ch 3 (96 sts).

Do not fasten off.

Round 7 (RS): using **yarn B**, sl st in next st, sl st in next 2-ch sp, ch 3, [1 dc, ch 2, 2 dc] in same sp; [using **yarn B**, 1 dc in each of next 2 sts; using **yarn C**, 1 dc in each of next 4 sts; (using **yarn B**, 1 dc in each of next 4 sts; using **yarn C**, 1 dc in each of next 4 sts) twice; using **yarn B**, 1 dc in each of next 2 sts, (2 dc, ch 2, 2 dc) in 2-ch sp] four times, omit [2 dc, ch 2, 2 dc] on last rep, sl st in third ch of beginning ch 3 (112 sts).

Fasten off **yarn B**.

Round 8 (RS): using **yarn A**, in 2-ch sp, ch 3, [1 dc, ch 2, 2 dc] in same sp; [using **yarn C**, 1 dc in each of next 4 sts; (using **yarn A**, 1 dc in each of next 4 sts; using **yarn C**, 1 dc in each of next 4 sts) three times; using **yarn A**, (2 dc, ch 2, 2 dc) in 2-ch sp] four times, omit [2 dc, ch 2, 2 dc] on last rep; using **yarn A**, sl st in third ch of beginning ch 3 (128 sts).

Do not fasten off.

Round 9 (RS): using **yarn A**, sl st in next st, sl st in next 2-ch sp, ch 3, [1 dc, ch 2, 2 dc] in same sp; [using **yarn A**, 1 dc in each of next 2 sts; using **yarn C**, 1 dc in each of next 4 sts; (using **yarn A**, 1 dc in each of next 4 sts; using **yarn

C**, 1 dc in each of next 4 sts) three times; using **yarn A**, 1 dc in each of next 2 sts, (2 dc, ch 2, 2 dc) in 2-ch sp] four times, omit [2 dc, ch 2, 2 dc] on last rep, sl st in third ch of beginning ch 3 (144 sts).

Fasten off **yarn A** and **yarn C**.

Weave in ends and block.

NOTE: From round 2 onward, you will need to switch between two shades at a time. One of these will always be **yarn C**. Do not fasten this off until instructed.

SKILL LEVEL

HOOK SIZE	BLOCK SIZE
US C/2 (3mm)	6 x 6in (15 x 15cm)

YARN/COLORS

Sample uses Scheepjes Softfun

A = Snow (#2412)

B = Deep Violet (#2515)

C = Dark Turquoise (#2511)

D = Apple (#2516)

E = Canary (#2518)

F = Pumpkin (#2651)

G = Candy Apple (#2410)

STITCHES

ch—chain

sl st—slip stitch

sc—single crochet

dc—double crochet

bl sl st—slip stitch worked in back loop only

fl dc—double crochet worked in front loop only

pc4—4 dc popcorn stitch (ch 1 to secure)

beg pc4—beginning 4 dc popcorn stitch: ch 3 (counts as 1 dc), 3 dc, then close as regular pc

MIX AND MATCH

Page 80 ✛ Page 60

CHART KEY

For symbol key, see page 122

Rainbow Popcorn

This raised stitch is so much fun once you get the hang of it.

Using **yarn A**, start with a magic ring.

Round 1 (RS): ch 1 (does not count as st throughout), 8 sc into ring, sl st in beginning sc (8 sts).

Round 2 (RS): ch 1, [1 sc, ch 3, 1 sc] in same st, [1 sc in next st, (1 sc, ch 3, 1 sc) in next st] four times, omit [1 sc, ch 3, 1 sc] on last rep, sl st in beginning sc (12 sts).

Fasten off **yarn A**.

Round 3 (RS): using **yarn B**, in any 3-ch sp, 1 beg pc4 in same sp, [ch 3, skip next st, 1 bl sl st in next st, ch 3, skip next st, 1 pc4 in 3-ch sp] four times, omit 1 pc4 on last rep, sl st in beg pc4 (4 pc4, 8 x 3-ch sp, 4 bl sl st).

Fasten off **yarn B**.

Round 4 (RS): using **yarn A**, in any pc4, ch 1, [(1 sc, ch 3, 1 sc) in pc4, 2 sc in next 3-ch sp, 1 fl dc in remaining loop of round 2 st, 2 sc in next 3-ch sp] four times, sl st in beginning sc (28 sts).

Fasten off **yarn A**.

Round 5 (RS): using **yarn C**, in any 3-ch sp, 1 beg pc4 in same sp, [ch 3, skip next st, 1 bl sl st in next st, ch 3, skip next st, 1 pc4 in fl dc, ch 3, skip next st, 1 bl sl st in next st, ch 3, skip next st, 1 pc4 in 3-ch sp] four times, omit 1 pc4 on last rep, sl st in beg pc4 (8 pc4, 16 x 3-ch sp, 8 bl sl st).

Fasten off **yarn C**.

Round 6 (RS): using **yarn A**, in any pc4, ch 1, [(1 sc, ch 3, 1 sc) in pc4, 2 sc in next 3-ch sp, 1 fl dc in remaining loop of round 4 st, 2 sc in next 3-ch sp, 1 sc in pc4, 2 sc in next 3-ch sp, 1 fl dc in remaining loop of round 4 st, 2 sc in next 3-ch sp] four times, sl st in beginning sc (52 sts).

Fasten off **yarn A**.

Round 7 (RS): using **yarn D**, in any 3-ch sp, 1 beg pc4 in same sp, [ch 3, skip next st, 1 bl sl st in next st, ch 3, skip next st, 1 pc4 in fl dc, ch 3, skip next 2 sts, 1 bl sl st in next st, ch 3, skip next 2 sts, 1 pc4 in fl dc, ch 3, skip next st, 1 bl sl st in next st, ch 3, skip next st, 1 pc4 in 3-ch sp] four times, omit 1 pc4 on last rep, sl st in beg pc4 (12 pc4, 24 x 3-ch sp, 12 bl sl st).

Fasten off **yarn D**.

Round 8 (RS): using **yarn A**, in any pc4, ch 1, [(1 sc, ch 3, 1 sc) in pc4, 2 sc in next 3-ch sp, (1 fl dc in remaining loop of round 6 st, 2 sc in next 3-ch sp, 1 sc in pc4, 2 sc in next 3-ch sp) twice, 1 fl dc in remaining loop of round 6 st, 2 sc in next 3-ch sp] four times, sl st in beginning sc (76 sts).

Fasten off **yarn A**.

Round 9 (RS): using **yarn E**, in any 3-ch sp, 1 beg pc4 in same sp, [ch 3, skip next st, 1 bl sl st in next st, ch 3, skip next st, (1 pc4 in fl dc, ch 3, skip next 2 sts, 1 bl sl st in next st, ch 3,

skip next 2 sts) twice, 1 pc4 in fl dc, ch 3, skip next st, 1 bl sl st in next st, ch 3, skip next st, 1 pc4 in 3-ch sp] four times, omit 1 pc4 on last rep, sl st in beg pc4 (16 pc4, 32 x 3-ch sp, 16 bl sl st).

Fasten off **yarn E**.

Round 10 (RS): using **yarn A**, in any pc4, ch 1, [(1 sc, ch 3, 1 sc) in pc4, 2 sc in next 3-ch sp, (1 fl dc in remaining loop of round 8 st, 2 sc in next 3-ch sp, 1 sc in pc4, 2 sc in next 3-ch sp) three times, 1 fl dc in remaining loop of round 8 st, 2 sc in next 3-ch sp] four times, sl st in beginning sc (100 sts).

Fasten off **yarn A**.

Round 11 (RS): using **yarn F**, in any 3-ch sp, 1 beg pc4 in same sp, [ch 3, skip next st, 1 bl sl st in next st, ch 3, skip next st, (1 pc4 in fl dc, ch 3, skip next 2 sts, 1 bl sl st in next st, ch 3, skip next 2 sts) three times, 1 pc4 in fl dc, ch 3, skip next st, 1 bl sl st in next st, ch 3, skip next st, 1 pc4 in 3-ch sp] four times, omit 1 pc4 on last rep, sl st in beg pc4 (20 pc4, 40 x 3-ch sp, 20 bl sl st).

Fasten off **yarn F**.

Round 12 (RS): using **yarn A**, in any pc4, ch 1, [(1 sc, ch 3, 1 sc) in pc4, 2 sc in next 3-ch sp, (1 fl dc in remaining loop of round 10 st, 2 sc in next 3-ch sp, 1 sc in pc4, 2 sc in next 3-ch sp) four times, 1 fl dc in remaining loop of round 10 st, 2 sc in next 3-ch sp] four times, sl st in beginning sc (124 sts).

Fasten off **yarn A**.

Round 13 (RS): using **yarn G**, in any 3-ch sp, 1 beg pc4 in same sp, [ch 3, skip next st, 1 bl sl st in next st, ch 3, skip next st, (1 pc4 in fl dc, ch 3, skip next 2 sts, 1 bl sl st in next st, ch 3, skip next 2 sts) four times, 1 pc4 in fl dc, ch 3, skip next st, 1 bl sl st in next st, ch 3, skip next

st, 1 pc4 in 3-ch sp] four times, omit 1 pc4 on last rep, sl st in beg pc4 (24 pc4, 48 x 3-ch sp, 24 bl sl st).

Fasten off **yarn G**.

Round 14 (RS): using **yarn A**, in any pc4, ch 1, [(1 sc, ch 3, 1 sc) in pc4, 2 sc in next 3-ch sp, (1 fl dc in remaining loop of round 12 st, 2 sc in next 3-ch sp, skip pc4, 2 sc in next 3-ch sp) five times, 1 fl dc in remaining loop of round 12 st, 2 sc in next 3-ch sp] four times, sl st in beginning sc (128 sts).

Round 15 (RS): sl st in 3-ch sp, ch 1, [3 sc in 3-ch sp, 1 sc in each of next 37 sts] four times, sl st in beginning sc (140 sts).

Fasten off **yarn A**.

Weave in ends and block.

NOTE: Due to the nature of the stitches in this square, blocking your final piece is essential for the best results.

HOOK SIZE	BLOCK SIZE
US E/4 (3.5mm)	6 x 6in (15 x 15cm)

YARN/COLORS
Sample uses Scheepjes Softfun
A = Butterscotch (#2610)
B = Snow (#2412)
C = Light Rose (#2513)
D = Rose (#2514)
E = Hot Pink (#2495)
F = Botanical (#2615)
G = Green Tea (#2639)

STITCHES
ch—chain
sl st—slip stitch
sc—single crochet
dc—double crochet
tr—treble crochet
bl sl st—slip stitch worked
in back loop only
bp sl st—back post
slip stitch

MIX AND MATCH

Page 99 + Page 38 + Page 20

CHART KEY
For symbol key, see page 122

Sugar Flower

A great way to try out making a crocheted flower in 3D.

Using yarn A, start with a magic ring.

Round 1 (RS): ch 1 (does not count as st throughout), 8 sc into ring, bl sl st in beginning sc (8 sts).

NOTE: Work next round in back loops only.

Round 2 (RS): ch 1, 2 sc in each st around, sl st in beginning sc (16 sts).

Fasten off yarn A.

NOTE: Work next round in remaining front loops of round 1.

Round 3 (RS): using yarn B, [1 sl st, ch 3, 1 dc, ch 3, 1 sl st] in each st around, sl st in beginning sl st (8 petals).

Fasten off yarn B.

Round 4 to be made in round 2.

Round 4 (RS): using yarn C, in any st, ch 1, 2 sc in same st, [1 sc in next st, 2 sc in next st] eight times, omit 2 sc on last rep, sl st in beginning sc (24 sts).

Round 5 to be made in round 4.

Round 5 (RS): ch 1, 2 sc in same st, [1 sc in each of next 2 sts, 2 sc in next st] eight times, omit 2 sc on last rep, sl st in beginning sc (32 sts).

Fasten off yarn C.

Round 6 to be made in round 5.

Round 6 (RS): using yarn D, sl st in any st,

[ch 3, skip next st, sl st in next st, ch 2, skip next st, sl st in next st] eight times, omit 1 sl st on last rep, sl st in beginning sl st (8 x 3-ch sp, 8 x 2-ch sp, 16 sl st).

Round 7 to be made in round 6.

Round 7 (RS): sl st in next 3-ch sp, ch 3 (counts as 1 dc throughout), 4 dc in same 3-ch sp, [sl st in next 2-ch sp, 5 dc in next 3-ch sp] eight times, omit 5 dc on last rep, sl st in third ch of beginning ch 3 (8 petals).

Fasten off **yarn D**.

NOTE: Work round 8 around stitches made in round 6.

Round 8 (RS): using **yarn E**, bp sl st around any round 6 sl st, ch 3, [bp sl st around next round 6 sl st, ch 3] fifteen times, sl st in beginning bp sl st (16 x 3-ch sp, 16 bp sl st).

Round 9 (RS): sl st in next 3-ch sp, ch 3, [3 tr, 1 dc] in same 3-ch sp, [1 sc in next 3-ch sp, (1 dc, 3 tr, 1 dc) in next 3-ch sp] eight times, omit [1 dc, 3 tr, 1 dc] on last rep, sl st in third ch of beginning ch 3 (8 petals).

Fasten off **yarn E**.

Round 10 (RS): using **yarn B**, bp sl st around any sc, ch 5, [bp sl st around next sc, ch 5] seven times, sl st in beginning bp sl st (8 x 5-ch sp, 8 bp sl st).

Round 11 (RS): sl st in next 5-ch sp, ch 4 (counts as 1 tr), [2 tr, ch 3, 3 tr] in same 5-ch sp, [ch 1, 3 dc in next 5-ch sp, ch 1, (3 tr, ch 3, 3 tr) in next 5-ch sp] four times, omit [3 tr, ch 3, 3 tr] on last rep, sl st in fourth ch of beginning ch 4 (24 tr, 12 dc, 4 x 3-ch sp, 8 x ch sp).

Fasten off **yarn B**.

Round 12 (RS): using **yarn F**, in any 3-ch sp, ch 3, [2 dc, ch 2, 3 dc] in same sp, [ch 1, (3 dc in next ch sp, ch 1) twice, (3 dc, ch 2, 3 dc) in next 3-ch sp] four times, omit [3 dc, ch 2, 3 dc] on last rep, sl st in third ch of beginning ch 3 (48 dc, 4 x 2-ch sp, 12 x ch sp).

Fasten off **yarn F**.

Round 13 (RS): using **yarn G**, in any 2-ch sp, ch 3, [2 dc, ch 2, 3 dc] in same sp, [ch 1, ({1 dc, ch 2, 1 dc} in next ch sp, ch 1) three times, (3 dc, ch 2, 3 dc) in next 2-ch sp] four times, omit [3 dc, ch 2, 3 dc] on last rep, sl st in third ch of beginning ch 3 (48 dc, 16 x 2-ch sp, 16 x ch sp).

Fasten off **yarn G**.

Round 14 (RS): using **yarn B**, in any corner 2-ch sp, ch 3, [2 dc, ch 2, 3 dc] in same sp, [ch 3, (3 dc in next 2-ch sp, ch 1) twice, 3 dc in next 2-ch sp, ch 3, (3 dc, ch 2, 3 dc) in corner 2-ch sp] four times, omit [3 dc, ch 2, 3 dc] on last rep, sl st in third ch of beginning ch 3 (60 dc, 8 x 3-ch sp, 4 x 2-ch sp, 8 x ch sp).

Fasten off **yarn B**.

Round 15 (RS): using **yarn C**, in any 2-ch sp, ch 1, [(1 sc, ch 2, 1 sc) in 2-ch sp, 1 sc in each of next 3 sts, 3 sc in 3-ch sp, (1 sc in each of next 3 sts, 1 sc in ch sp) twice, 1 sc in each of next 3 sts, 3 sc in 3-ch sp, 1 sc in each of next 3 sts] four times, sl st in beginning sc (100 sts).

Fasten off **yarn C**.

Round 16 (RS): using **yarn D**, in any 2-ch sp, ch 1, [(1 sc, ch 2, 1 sc) in 2-ch sp, 1 sc in each of next 25 sts] four times, sl st in beginning sc (108 sts).

Fasten off **yarn D**.

Round 17 (RS): using **yarn B**, in any 2-ch sp, ch 1, [3 sc in 2-ch sp, 1 sc in each of next 27 sts] four times, sl st in beginning sc (120 sts).

Fasten off **yarn B**.

Weave in ends and block.

3D Heart

Popcorn stitch creates a raised heart and a delicate scalloped edge mimics a lacy border.

———

Using **yarn A**, start with a magic ring.

Round 1 (RS): 1 beg pc5, ch 3, [1 pc5, ch 3 into ring] three times, sl st in beg pc5 (4 pc5, 4 x 3-ch sp).

Round 2 (RS): sl st in 3-ch sp, [1 beg pc5, ch 3, 1 pc5] in same sp, ch 2, [1 pc5, ch 3, 1 pc5] in next 3-ch sp, ch 2] three times, sl st in beg pc5 (8 pc5, 4 x 3-ch sp, 4 x 2-ch sp).

Round 3 (RS): sl st in 3-ch sp, [1 beg pc5, ch 3,1 pc5] in same sp, ch 2, 1 pc5 in next 2-ch sp; using **yarn B**, ch 5, [sl st, ch 7, sl st] in 3-ch sp, ch 4; using **yarn A** (join/change of color to be counted as ch 1), 1 pc5 in next 2-ch sp; using **yarn B**, ch 5, [sl st, ch 7, sl st] in 3-ch sp, ch 4; using **yarn A**, 1 pc5 in next 2-ch sp, ch 2, [1 pc5, ch 3, 1 pc5] in 3-ch sp; using **yarn B**, ch 5, 1 sc in next 2-ch sp, ch 4; using **yarn A**, sl st in beg pc5 (7 pc5, 6 x 5-ch sp, 2 x 7-ch sp, 2 x 3-ch sp, 2 x 2-ch sp, 1 sc).

Round 4 (RS): sl st in 3-ch sp, (1 beg pc5, ch 5, 1 pc5) in same sp, ch 2, 1 pc5 in next 2-ch sp; using **yarn B**, ch 5, 1 sc in next 5-ch sp, ch 5, [sl st, ch 7, sl st] in 7-ch sp, [ch 5, 1 sc in next 5-ch sp] twice, ch 5, [sl st, ch 7, sl st] in 7-ch sp, ch 5, 1 sc in next 5-ch sp, ch 4; using **yarn A**, 1 pc5 in next 2-ch sp, ch 2, (1 pc5, ch 5, 1 pc5) in next 3-ch sp; using **yarn B**, [ch 5, 1 sc in next 5-ch sp] twice, ch 5, sl st in beg pc5 (6 pc5, 12 x 5-ch sp, 2 x 7-ch sp, 2 x 2-ch sp, 6 sc).

Fasten off **yarn A**.

Round 5 (RS): sl st in 5-ch sp, [ch 7, sl st] in same sp, ch 5, 1 sc in next 2-ch sp, [ch 5, 1 sc in next 5-ch sp] twice, ch 5, [sl st, ch 7, sl st] in 7-ch sp, [ch 5, 1 sc in next 5-ch sp] three

times, ch 5, [sl st, ch 7, sl st] in 7-ch sp, [ch 5, 1 sc in next 5-ch sp] twice, ch 5, 1 sc in next 2-ch sp, ch 5, [sl st, ch 7, sl st] in next 5-ch sp, [ch 5, 1 sc in next 5-ch sp] three times, ch 5 (16 x 5-ch sp, 4 x 7-ch sp, 12 sc).

Do not fasten off.

Round 6 (RS): sl st in next 7-ch sp, [ch 7, sl st] in same sp, [ch 5, (1 sc in next 5-ch sp, ch 5) four times, (sl st, ch 7, sl st) in 7-ch sp] four times, omit [sl st, ch 7, sl st] on last rep (20 x 5-ch sp, 4 x 7-ch sp, 16 sc).

Do not fasten off.

Round 7 (RS): sl st in next 7-ch sp, [ch 5, sl st] in same sp, [ch 3, (1 sc in next 5-ch sp, ch 3) five times, (sl st, ch 5, sl st) in 7-ch sp] four times, omit [sl st, ch 5, sl st] on last rep (4 x 5-ch sp, 24 x 3-ch sp, 20 sc).

Do not fasten off.

Round 8 (RS): sl st in next 5-ch sp, ch 2 (does not count as st) [5 hdc in 5-ch sp, 3 hdc in next 3-ch sp, (1 sc next sc, 3 hdc in next 3-ch sp) five times] four times, sl st in beginning hdc (112 sts).

Fasten off **yarn B**.

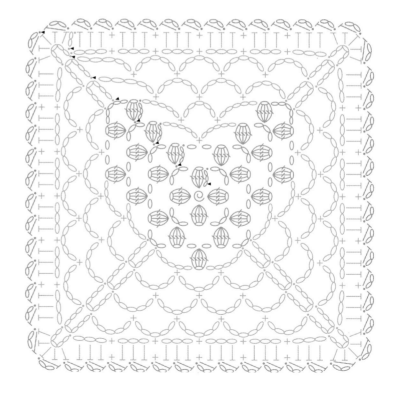

SCALLOP EDGE

Round 9 (RS): using **yarn C**, in third hdc of any 5 hdc group, ch 2, 1 hdc in same st, skip next st, [[(1 sl st, ch 2, 1 hdc) in next st, skip next st] fifty-five times, sl st in beginning join (56 shells).

Fasten off **yarn C**.

Weave in ends and block.

NOTES: Throughout rounds 3–5 you will need to switch between **yarn A** and **yarn B**. Do not fasten off either until instructed. Join/change of color after a pc stitch to be counted as ch 1 used to secure. Join/change of color before a pc stitch to be counted as ch 1.

HOOK SIZE	BLOCK SIZE
US G/6 (4mm)	6 x 6in (15 x 15cm)

TECHNIQUES
Changing color on row/round (see page 121)
Working into round/row ends (see page 125)
Working over/into previous rounds/rows
(see page 119)

YARN/COLORS
Sample uses Scheepjes Softfun

A = Light Rose (#2513)	F = Botanical (#2615)
B = Rose (#2514)	G = Cool Blue (#2603)
C = Cantaloupe (#2652)	H = Bright Turquoise (#2423)
D = Canary (#2518)	I = Orchid (#2657)
E = Mint (#2640)	J = Snow (#2412)

STITCHES
ch—chain
sl st—slip stitch
sc—single crochet
dc—double crochet
fptr—front post treble crochet

MIX AND MATCH

Page 42 **+** Page 78

CHART KEY
For symbol key, see page 122

Pastel Grid
A great block for trying out ombré effects.

Using **yarn A**, start with a magic ring.
Round 1 (RS): ch 3 (counts as 1 dc throughout), 2 dc into ring, ch 2, [3 dc, ch 2 into ring] three times, sl st in third ch of beginning ch 3 (12 sts).
Fasten off **yarn A**.
Round 2 (RS): using **yarn B**, in any 2-ch sp, [ch 3, 2 dc, ch 2, 3 dc] in same sp, [skip next 3 sts, (3 dc, ch 2, 3 dc) in next 2-ch sp] three times, sl st in third ch of beginning ch 3 (24 sts).

Fasten off **yarn B**.
Row 3 (RS): using **yarn C**, in any 2-ch sp, [ch 3, 2 dc] in same sp, skip next 3 sts, 1 dc in st sp, 1 fptr around round 1 dc directly below, 1 dc in same st sp, skip next 3 sts, [3 dc, ch 2, 3 dc] in 2-ch sp, skip next 3 sts, 1 dc in st sp, 1 fptr around round 1 dc directly below, 1 dc in same st sp, skip next 3 sts, 3 dc in 2-ch sp, turn (18 sts).
Row 4 (WS): ch 3, skip next 2 sts, [3 dc in st sp, skip next 3 sts] twice, [3 dc, ch 2, 3 dc] in

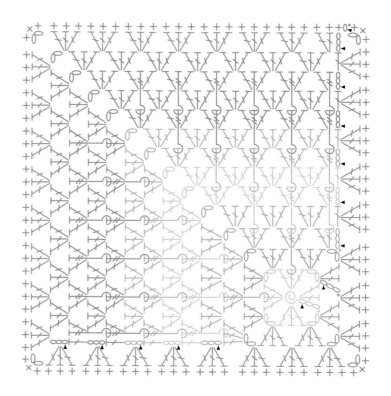

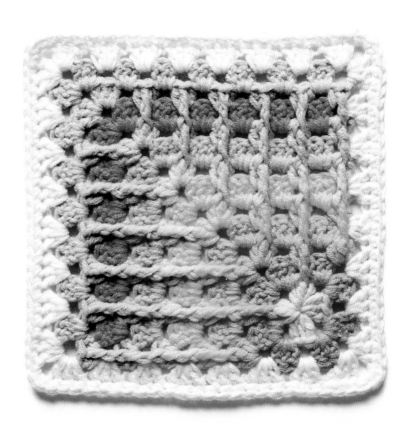

2-ch sp, [skip next 3 sts, 3 dc in st sp] twice, skip next 2 sts, 1 dc in last st, join **yarn D**, turn (20 sts).

Fasten off **yarn C**.

Row 5 (RS): ch 3, 1 fptr around row 3 dc directly below, 1 dc in st sp, skip next 3 sts, 1 dc in st sp, 1 fptr around row 3 fptr, 1 dc in same st sp, skip next 3 sts, 1 dc in st sp, 1 fptr around row 3 dc directly below, 1 dc in same st sp, skip next 3 sts, [3 dc, ch 2, 3 dc] in 2-ch sp, skip next 3 sts, 1 dc in st sp, 1 fptr around row 3 dc directly below, 1 dc in same st sp, skip next 3 sts, 1 dc in st sp, 1 fptr around row 3 fptr, 1 dc in same st sp, skip next 3 sts, 1 dc in st sp, 1 fptr around row 3 dc directly below, 1 dc in same st sp, turn (24 sts).

Row 6 (WS): ch 3, skip next 2 sts, [3 dc in st sp, skip next 3 sts] three times, [3 dc, ch 2, 3 dc] in 2-ch sp, [skip next 3 sts, 3 dc in st sp] three times, skip next 2 sts, 1 dc in last st, join **yarn E**, turn (26 sts).

Fasten off **yarn D**.

Row 7 (RS): ch 3, 1 fptr around row 5 dc directly below, 1 dc in st sp, skip next 3 sts, [1 dc in st sp, 1 fptr around row 5 fptr, 1 dc in same st sp, skip next 3 sts] twice, 1 dc in st sp, 1 fptr around row 5 dc directly below, 1 dc in same st sp, skip next 3 sts, [3 dc, ch 2, 3 dc] in 2-ch sp, skip next 3 sts, 1 dc in st sp, 1 fptr around row 5 dc directly below, 1 dc in same st sp, [skip next 3 sts, 1 dc in st sp, 1 fptr around row 5 fptr, 1 dc in same st sp] three times, join **yarn F**, turn (30 sts).

Fasten off **yarn E**.

Row 8 (WS): ch 3, skip next 2 sts, [3 dc in st sp, skip next 3 sts] four times, [3 dc, ch 2, 3 dc] in 2-ch sp, [skip next 3 sts, 3 dc in st sp] four times, skip next 2 sts, 1 dc in last st, join **yarn G**, turn (32 sts).

Fasten off **yarn F**.

Row 9 (RS): ch 3, 1 fptr around row 7 fptr, 1 dc in st sp, skip next 3 sts, [1 dc in st sp, 1 fptr around row 7 fptr, 1 dc in same st sp, skip next 3 sts] three times, 1 dc in st sp, 1 fptr around row 7 dc directly below, 1 dc in same st sp, skip next 3 sts, [3 dc, ch 2, 3 dc] in 2-ch sp, skip next 3 sts, 1 dc in st sp, 1 fptr around row 7 dc directly below, 1 dc in same st sp, [skip next 3 sts, 1 dc in st sp, 1 fptr around row 7 fptr, 1 dc in same st sp] four times, join **yarn H**, turn (36 sts).

Fasten off **yarn G**.

Row 10 (WS): ch 3, skip next 2 sts, [3 dc in st sp, skip next 3 sts] five times, [3 dc, ch 2, 3 dc] in 2-ch sp, [skip next 3 sts, 3 dc in st sp] five times, skip next 2 sts, 1 dc in last st, join **yarn I**, turn (38 sts).

Fasten off **yarn H**.

Row 11 (RS): ch 3, 1 fptr around row 9 fptr, 1 dc in st sp, skip next 3 sts, [1 dc in st sp, 1 fptr around row 9 fptr, 1 dc in same st sp, skip next 3 sts] four times, 1 dc in st sp, 1 fptr around row 9 dc directly below, 1 dc in same st sp, skip next 3 sts, [3 dc, ch 2, 3 dc] in 2-ch sp, skip next 3 sts, 1 dc in st sp, 1 fptr around row 9 dc directly below, 1 dc in same st sp, [skip next 3 sts, 1 dc in st sp, 1 fptr around row 9 fptr, 1 dc in same st sp] five times, turn (42 sts).

Row 12 (WS): ch 3, skip next 2 sts, [3 dc in st sp, skip next 3 sts] six times, [3 dc, ch 2, 3 dc] in 2-ch sp, [skip next 3 sts, 3 dc in st sp] six times, skip next 2 sts, 1 dc in last st, join **yarn J**, turn (44 sts).

Fasten off **yarn I**.

Round 13 (RS): sl st in next st sp, [ch 3, 2 dc] in same sp, skip next 3 sts, [3 dc in st sp, skip next 3 sts] six times, [3 dc, ch 2, 3 dc] in 2-ch sp, skip next 3 sts, [3 dc in st sp, skip next 3 sts] six times, 3 dc in st sp, ch 2, 3 dc in side of row 12, 3 dc in side of row 10, 3 dc in side of row 8, 3 dc in side of row 6, 3 dc in side of row 4, 3 dc in ch sp, skip next 3 sts, 3 dc in st sp, skip next 3 sts, [3 dc, ch 2, 3 dc] in 2-ch sp, skip next 3 sts, 3 dc in st sp, 3 dc in ch sp, 3 dc in side of row 4, 3 dc in side of row 6, 3 dc in side of row 8, 3 dc in side of row 10, 3 dc in side of row 12, ch 2, sl st in third ch of beginning ch 3 (96 sts).

Round 14 (RS): ch 1 (does not count as st), 1 sc in same st, 1 sc in each of next 23 sts, 3 sc in 2-ch sp, [1 sc in each of next 24 sts, 3 sc in 2-ch sp] three times, sl st in beginning sc (108 sc).

Fasten off **yarn J**.

Weave in ends and block.

HOOK SIZE	BLOCK SIZE
US E/4 (3.5mm)	6 x 6in (15 x 15cm)

TECHNIQUES
Working with multiple colors at the same time/ intarsia crochet (see page 121)

Changing color on row/round (see page 121)

Working over/into previous rounds/rows (see page 119)

YARN/COLORS
Sample uses Scheepjes Softfun

A = Snow (#2412)

B = Canary (#2518)

C = Hot Pink (#2495)

D = Botanical (#2615)

STITCHES

ch—chain	dc—double crochet
sl st—slip stitch	tr—treble crochet
sc—single crochet	fptrtr—front post triple treble crochet
hdc—half double crochet	

MIX AND MATCH

Page 38 ✛ Page 89

CHART KEY
For symbol key, see page 122

Citrus Slice

See page 106 for a creative way to use this block in a project.

———

Using **yarn A**, start with a magic ring.

Round 1 (RS): ch 3 (counts as 1 hdc, ch 1), [1 hdc, ch 1 into ring] seven times, sl st in second ch of beginning ch 3 (8 sts). Fasten off **yarn A**.

Round 2 (RS): using **yarn B**, in any ch sp, ch 2 (does not count as st throughout), 2 hdc in each ch sp around, sl st in beginning hdc (16 sts).

Round 3 (RS): ch 2, 2 hdc in same st, [1 hdc in next st, 2 hdc in next st] eight times, omit 2 hdc on last rep, sl st in beginning hdc (24 sts).

Round 4 (RS): ch 2, 2 hdc in same st, [1 hdc in each of next 2 sts, 2 hdc in next st] eight times, omit 2 hdc on last rep, sl st in beginning hdc (32 sts).

Round 5 (RS): ch 2, 2 hdc in same st, [1 hdc in each of next 3 sts, 2 hdc in next st] eight times, omit 2 hdc on last rep, sl st in beginning hdc (40 sts). Fasten off **yarn B**.

Round 6 (RS): using **yarn A**, in first st made in round 5, ch 1 (does not count as st throughout), 1 sc in same st, [1 sc in each

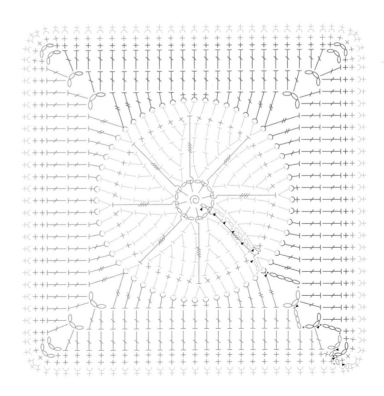

of next 4 sts, 1 fptrtr around round 1 hdc directly below, 1 sc in next st] eight times, omit 1 sc on last rep, sl st in beginning sc (48 sts).

Fasten off **yarn A**.

Round 7 (RS): using **yarn B**, in any fptrtr, ch 2, 2 hdc in same st, [1 hdc in each of next 5 sts, 2 hdc in next st] eight times, omit 2 hdc on last rep, sl st in beginning hdc (56 sts).

Fasten off **yarn B**.

All sts in next round to be made in back loop only.

Round 8 (RS): using **yarn C**, in first st made in round 7, ch 4 (counts as 1 tr), 1 tr in next st, 1 dc in each of next 2 sts, 1 hdc in each of next 2 sts, 1 sc in each of next 3 sts, 1 hdc in each of next 2 sts, 1 dc in each of next 2 sts, 1 tr in next st, [1 tr, ch 3, 1 tr] in next st, 1 tr in next st, 1 dc in each of next 2 sts, 1 hdc in each of next 2 sts, 1 sc in each of next 3 sts, 1 hdc in each of next 2 sts, 1 dc in each of next 2 sts, 1 tr in next st, 1 tr in next st, ch 1; using **yarn D** (join/change of color to be counted as ch 1 throughout), ch 1, 1 tr in same st, 1 tr in next st, 1 dc in each of next 2 sts, 1 hdc in each of next 2 sts, 1 sc in each of next 3 sts, 1 hdc in each of next 2 sts, 1 dc in each of next 2 sts, 1 tr in next st, [1 tr, ch 3, 1 tr] in next st, 1 tr in next st, 1 dc in each of next 2 sts, 1 hdc in each of next 2 sts, 1 sc in

each of next 3 sts, 1 hdc in each of next 2 sts, 1 dc in each of next 2 sts, 1 tr in next st, 1 tr in next st (this will be the same round 7 st as one started at beginning of this round), ch 3, sl st in fourth ch of beginning ch 4, turn (60 sts).

Round 9 (WS): using **yarn D**, loosely sl st back in 3-ch sp, [ch 3, 1 dc] in same sp, 1 dc in each of next 15 sts, [2 dc, ch 3, 2 dc] in 3-ch sp, 1 dc in each of next 15 sts, 2 dc in 3-ch sp, ch 1; using **yarn C**, ch 1, 2 dc in same sp, 1 dc in each of next 15 sts, [2 dc, ch 3, 2 dc] in 3-ch sp, 1 dc in each of next 15 sts, 2 dc in 3-ch sp, ch 3, sl st in third ch of beginning ch 3, turn (76 sts).

Round 10 (RS): using **yarn C**, loosely sl st back in 3-ch sp, [ch 3, 1 dc] in same sp, 1 dc in each of next 19 sts, [2 dc, ch 3, 2 dc] in 3-ch sp, 1 dc in each of next 19 sts, 2 dc in 3-ch sp, ch 1; using **yarn D**, ch 1, 2 dc in same sp, 1 dc in each of next 19 sts, [2 dc, ch 3, 2 dc] in 3-ch sp, 1 dc in each of next 19 sts, 2 dc in 3-ch sp, ch 3, sl st in third ch of beginning ch 3, turn (92 sts).

Round 11 (WS): using **yarn D**, loosely sl st back in 3-ch sp, ch 1, 1 sc in same sp, 1 sc in each of next 23 sts, [1 sc, ch 3, 1 sc] in 3-ch sp, 1 sc in each of next 23 sts, 1 sc in 3-ch sp, ch 1; using **yarn C**, ch 1, 1 sc in same sp, 1 sc in each of next 23 sts, [1 sc, ch 3, 1 sc] in 3-ch

sp, 1 sc in each of next 23 sts, 1 sc in 3-ch sp, ch 3, sl st in beginning sc, turn (100 sts).

Fasten off **yarn C** and **yarn D**.

Round 12 (RS): using **yarn A**, in any 3-ch sp, ch 1, [3 sc in 3-ch sp, 1 sc in each of next 25 sts] four times, sl st in beginning sc (112 sts).

Fasten off **yarn A**.

All sts in next round to be made in back loop only.

Round 13 (RS): using **yarn B**, in second sc of any 3 sc corner group, ch 1, 3 sc in same st, [1 sc in each of next 27 sts, 3 sc in next st] four times, omit 3 sc on last rep, sl st in beginning sc (120 sts).

Fasten off **yarn B**.

Weave in ends and block.

NOTE: Rounds 7–11 require you to work with two different colors of yarn within a single round using a method called intarsia. Do not fasten off any colors until instructed.

Bright Shimmer

An essential to have in your crochet pattern collection; see page 38 for a plain version.

Using **yarn A**, start with a magic ring.

Round 1 (WS): ch 3 (counts as 1 dc throughout), 2 dc into ring, ch 2, [3 dc, ch 2 into ring] three times, sl st in third ch of beginning ch 3, turn (12 sts).

Fasten off **yarn A.**

Round 2 (RS): using **yarn B**, in any 2-ch sp, [ch 3, 2 dc, ch 2, 3 dc] in same sp, [skip next 3 sts, (3 dc, ch 2, 3 dc) in next 2-ch sp] three times, sl st in third ch of beginning ch 3, turn (24 sts).

Fasten off **yarn B.**

Round 3 (WS): using **yarn C**, in any 2-ch sp, [ch 3, 2 dc, ch 2, 3 dc] in same sp, [skip next 3 sts, 3 dc in next st sp, (3 dc, ch 2, 3 dc) in next 2-ch sp] four times, omit [3 dc, ch 2, 3 dc] on last rep, sl st in third ch of beginning ch 3, turn (36 sts).

Fasten off **yarn C.**

Round 4 (RS): using **yarn D**, in any 2-ch sp, [ch 3, 2 dc, ch 2, 3 dc] in same sp, [skip next 3 sts, (3 dc in next st sp, skip next 3 sts) twice, (3 dc, ch 2, 3 dc) in next 2-ch sp] four times, omit [3 dc, ch 2, 3 dc] on last rep, sl st in third ch of beginning ch 3, turn (48 sts).

Fasten off **yarn D.**

Round 5 (WS): using **yarn E**, in any 2-ch sp, [ch 3, 2 dc, ch 2, 3 dc] in same sp, [skip next 3 sts, (3 dc in next st sp, skip next 3 sts) three times, (3 dc, ch 2, 3 dc) in next 2-ch sp] four times, omit [3 dc, ch 2, 3 dc] on last rep, sl st in third ch of beginning ch 3, turn (60 sts).

Fasten off **yarn E.**

Round 6 (RS): using **yarn F**, in any 2-ch sp, [ch 3, 2 dc, ch 2, 3 dc] in same sp, [skip next 3 sts, (3 dc in next st sp, skip next 3 sts) four times, (3 dc, ch 2, 3 dc) in next 2-ch sp] four times, omit [3 dc, ch 2, 3 dc] on last rep, sl st in third ch of beginning ch 3, turn (72 sts).

Fasten off **yarn F.**

Round 7 (WS): using **yarn G**, in any 2-ch sp, [ch 3, 2 dc, ch 2, 3 dc] in same sp, [skip next 3 sts, (3 dc in next st sp, skip next 3 sts) five times, (3 dc, ch 2, 3 dc) in next 2-ch sp] four times, omit [3 dc, ch 2, 3 dc] on last rep, sl st in third ch of beginning ch 3, turn (84 sts).

Fasten off **yarn G.**

Round 8 (RS): using **yarn H**, in any 2-ch sp, [ch 3, 2 dc, ch 2, 3 dc] in same sp, [skip next 3 sts, (3 dc in next st sp, skip next 3 sts) six times, (3 dc, ch 2, 3 dc) in next 2-ch sp] four times, omit [3 dc, ch 2, 3 dc] on last rep, sl st in third ch of beginning ch 3 (96 sts).

Fasten off **yarn H.**

Weave in ends and block.

SKILL LEVEL

HOOK SIZE	BLOCK SIZE
US G/6 (4mm)	6 x 6in (15 x 15cm)

YARN/COLORS
Sample uses Scheepjes Softfun
A = Deep Violet (#2515)
B = Bright Turquoise (#2423)
C = Apple (#2516)
D = Canary (#2518)
E = Tangerine (#2427)
F = Candy Apple (#2410)
G = Rose (#2514)
H = Snow (#2412)

STITCHES
ch—chain
sl st—slip stitch
dc—double crochet

MIX AND MATCH

Page 92 + Page 50

CHART KEY
For symbol key, see page 122

NOTES: The majority of this square is worked in the spaces between stitches. Do not work directly into a stitch unless otherwise instructed.
A flat square is achieved by alternating the sides each round is worked on: odd rounds are worked on WS; even rounds on RS.

For even better results, begin each round in the corner directly opposite to the one in the previous round.

Double Crochet Square

A single-color block that is ideal for combining with more detailed blocks.

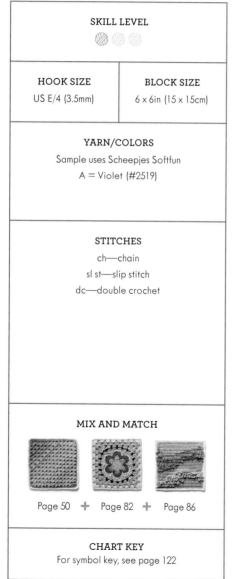

SKILL LEVEL
◍ ◌ ◌

HOOK SIZE	BLOCK SIZE
US E/4 (3.5mm)	6 x 6in (15 x 15cm)

YARN/COLORS

Sample uses Scheepjes Softfun
A = Violet (#2519)

STITCHES

ch—chain
sl st—slip stitch
dc—double crochet

MIX AND MATCH

Page 50 ✛ Page 82 ✛ Page 86

CHART KEY

For symbol key, see page 122

Using **yarn A**, start with a magic ring.
Round 1 (RS): ch 5 (counts as 1 dc, ch 2),
[3 dc, ch 2 into ring] three times, 2 dc into
ring, sl st in third ch of beginning ch 5 (12 sts).
Round 2 (RS): sl st in next 2-ch sp, ch 3
(counts as 1 dc throughout), [1 dc, ch 2, 2 dc]
in same 2-ch sp, 1 dc in each of next 3 sts,
[(2 dc, ch 2, 2 dc) in next 2-ch sp, 1 dc in each
of next 3 sts] three times, sl st in third ch of
beginning ch 3 (28 sts).
Rounds 3–8 (RS): sl st in next st, sl st in next
2-ch sp, ch 3, [1 dc, ch 2, 2 dc] in same

2-ch sp, 1 dc in each st until next 2-ch sp,
[(2 dc, ch 2, 2 dc) in 2-ch sp, 1 dc in each st
until next 2-ch sp] three times, sl st in third ch
of beginning ch 3 (124 sts).
Fasten off **yarn A**.

Weave in ends and block.

NOTE: From round 3, first sl st made in order
to get to first 2-ch sp is made to create a
seamless look.

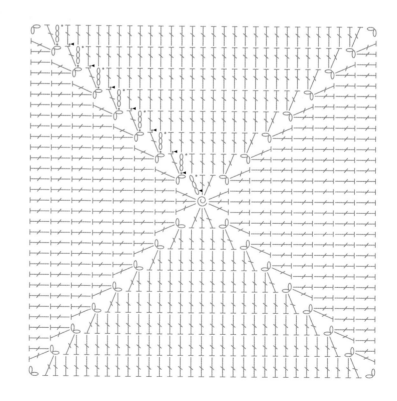

HOOK SIZE	BLOCK SIZE
US E/4 (3.5mm)	6 x 6in (15 x 15cm)

TECHNIQUES

Working with multiple colors at the same time/
intarsia crochet (see page 121)

Changing color on row/round (see page 121)

YARN/COLORS

Sample uses Scheepjes Softfun

A = Botanical (#2615)

B = Soft Coral (#2636)

C = Canary (#2518)

D = Orchid (#2657)

E = Snow (#2412)

STITCHES

ch—chain

sl st—slip stitch

sc—single crochet

dc—double crochet

MIX AND MATCH

Page 72 + Page 22 + Page 30

CHART KEY

For symbol key, see page 122

Intarsia Triangles

This block creates an interesting diagonal pattern.

Using **yarn A**, start with a magic ring.

Round 1 (RS): ch 3 (counts as 1 dc throughout), 2 dc into ring, ch 3, 3 dc into ring, ch 1; using **yarn B** (this join/change of color to be counted as ch 1 throughout), ch 1, [3 dc, ch 3 into ring] twice, sl st in third ch of beginning ch 3, turn (12 sts).

Round 2 (WS): using **yarn B**, loosely sl st back in 3-ch sp, [ch 3, 1 dc] in same sp, 1 dc in each of next 3 sts, [2 dc, ch 3, 2 dc] in 3-ch sp, 1 dc in each of next 3 sts, 2 dc in 3-ch sp, ch 1; using **yarn A**, ch 1, 3 dc in same sp, ch 1, skip next 3 sts, [3 dc, ch 3, 3 dc] in 3-ch sp, ch 1, skip next 3 sts, 3 dc in 3-ch sp, ch 3, sl st in third ch of beginning ch 3, turn (28 sts).

Round 3 (RS): using **yarn A**, loosely sl st back in 3-ch sp, [ch 3, 2 dc] in same sp, ch 1, skip next 3 sts, 3 dc in ch sp, ch 1, skip next 3 sts, [3 dc, ch 3, 3 dc] in 3-ch sp, ch 1, skip next 3 sts, 3 dc in ch sp, ch 1, skip next 3 sts, 3 dc in 3-ch sp, ch 1; using **yarn B**, ch 1, 2 dc in same sp, 1 dc in each of next 7 sts, [2 dc, ch 3, 2 dc] in 3-ch sp,

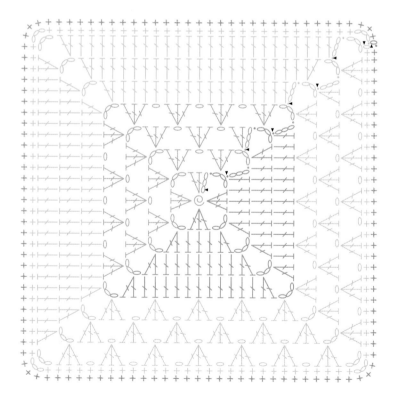

1 dc in each of next 7 sts, 2 dc in 3-ch sp, ch 3, sl st in third ch of beginning ch 3, turn (44 sts).

Round 4 (WS): using **yarn B,** loosely sl st back in 3-ch sp, [ch 3, 1 dc] in same sp, 1 dc in each of next 11 sts, [2 dc, ch 3, 2 dc] in 3-ch sp, 1 dc in each of next 11 sts, 2 dc in 3-ch sp, ch 1; using **yarn A,** ch 1, 3 dc in same sp, ch 1, skip next 3 sts, [3 dc in ch sp, ch 1, skip next 3 sts] twice, [3 dc, ch 3, 3 dc] in 3-ch sp, ch 1, skip next 3 sts, [3 dc in ch sp, ch 1, skip next 3 sts] twice, 3 dc in 3-ch sp, ch 3, sl st in third ch of beginning ch 3, turn (60 sts).

Fasten off **yarn A** and **yarn B.**

Round 5 (RS): using **yarn C,** in last 3-ch sp made in round 4, [ch 3, 1 dc] in same sp, 1 dc in each of next 3 sts, [1 dc in ch sp, 1 dc in each of next 3 sts] three times, [2 dc, ch 3, 2 dc] in 3-ch sp, 1 dc in each of next 3 sts, [1 dc in ch sp, 1 dc in each of next 3 sts] three times, 2 dc in 3-ch sp, ch 1; using **yarn D,** ch 1, 3 dc in same sp, ch 1, skip next 3 sts, [3 dc in next st, ch 1, skip next 3 sts] three times, [3 dc, ch 3, 3 dc] in 3-ch sp, ch 1, skip next 3 sts, [3 dc in next st, ch 1, skip next 3 sts] three times, 3 dc in 3-ch sp, ch 3, sl st in third ch of beginning ch 3, turn (76 sts).

Round 6 (WS): using **yarn D,** loosely sl st back in 3-ch sp, [ch 3, 2 dc] in same sp, ch 1, skip next 3 sts, [3 dc in ch sp, ch 1, skip next 3 sts] four times, [3 dc, ch 3, 3 dc] in 3-ch sp, ch 1, skip next 3 sts, [3 dc in next st, ch 1, skip next 3 sts] four times, 3 dc in 3-ch sp, ch 1; using **yarn C,** ch 1, 2 dc in same sp, 1 dc in each of next 19 sts, [2 dc, ch 3, 2 dc] in 3-ch sp, 1 dc in each of next 19 sts, 2 dc in 3-ch sp, ch 3, sl st in third ch of beginning ch 3, turn (92 sts).

Round 7 (RS): using **yarn C,** loosely sl st back in 3-ch sp, [ch 3, 1 dc] in same sp, 1 dc in each

of next 23 sts, [2 dc, ch 3, 2 dc] in 3-ch sp, 1 dc in each of next 23 sts, 2 dc in 3-ch sp, ch 1; using **yarn D,** ch 1, 3 dc in same sp, ch 1, skip next 3 sts, [3 dc in next st, ch 1, skip next 3 sts] five times, [3 dc, ch 3, 3 dc] in 3-ch sp, ch 1, skip next 3 sts, [3 dc in next st, ch 1, skip next 3 sts] five times, 3 dc in 3-ch sp, ch 3, sl st in third ch of beginning ch 3, turn (108 sts).

Round 8 (WS): using **yarn D,** loosely sl st back in 3-ch sp, ch 1 (does not count as st), 1 sc in same sp, 1 sc in each of next 3 sts, [1 sc in ch sp, 1 sc in each of next 3 sts] six times, [1 sc, ch 3, 1 sc] in 3-ch sp, 1 sc in each of next 3 sts, [1 sc in ch sp, 1 sc in each of

next 3 sts] six times, 1 sc in 3-ch sp, ch 1; using **yarn C,** ch 1, 1 sc in same sp, 1 sc in each of next 27 sts, [1 sc, ch 3, 1 sc] in 3-ch sp, 1 sc in each of next 27 sts, 1 sc in 3-ch sp, ch 3, sl st in third ch of beginning ch 3, turn (116 sts).

Fasten off **yarn C** and **yarn D.**

Round 9 (RS): using **yarn E,** in any 3-ch sp, ch 1 (does not count as st), [3 sc in 3-ch sp, 1 sc in each of next 29 sts] four times, sl st in beginning sc (128 sts).

Fasten off **yarn E.**

Weave in ends and block.

Modern Floral

A beautiful flower block that is a great way to try out some new stitches.

Using **yarn A**, start with a magic ring.

Round 1 (RS): ch 3 (counts as 1 dc throughout), 15 dc into ring, sl st in third ch of beginning ch 3 (16 sts).

Fasten off **yarn A**.

Round 2 (RS): using **yarn B**, in any st, [ch 4, tr-3-cl in next st, ch 4, sl st in next st] eight times (8 petals).

Fasten off **yarn B**.

Round 3 (RS): using **yarn C**, in any tr-3-cl, ch 1 (does not count as st throughout), 1 sc in same st, [ch 3, 1 fptr around round 1 dc between tr-cl, ch 3, 1 sc in next tr-3-cl] eight times, omit 1 sc on last rep, sl st in beginning sc (16 sts, 16 x 3-ch sp).

Fasten off **yarn C**.

Round 4 (RS): using **yarn D**, in any sc, ch 1, 1 sc in same st, [ch 2, 1 dc in fptr, ch 2, 1 sc in sc] eight times, omit 1 sc on last rep, sl st in beginning sc (16 sts, 16 x 2-ch sp).

Fasten off **yarn D**.

Round 5 (RS): using **yarn E**, in any 2-ch sp, [ch 3, 2 dc] in same sp, ch 1, skip next st, [3 dc in next 2-ch sp, ch 1, skip next st] fifteen times, sl st in third ch of beginning ch 3 (48 sts, 16 x ch sp).

Fasten off **yarn E**.

Round 6 (RS): using **yarn F**, in any ch sp, [ch 3, 1 dc, ch 2, 2 dc] in same sp, skip next 3 sts, [[2 dc, ch 2, 2 dc] in next ch sp, skip next 3 sts] fifteen times, sl st in third ch of beginning ch 3 (64 sts, 16 x 2-ch sp).

Fasten off **yarn F**.

Round 7 (RS): using **yarn G**, in any 2-ch sp, [sl st in 2-ch sp, skip next 4 sts, 11 dc in next 2-ch sp, skip next 4 sts] eight times, sl st in beginning sl st (8 x 11-dc petals).

Fasten off **yarn G**.

Round 8 (RS): using **yarn B**, in fourth dc of any 11-dc petal, ch 1, 1 sc in same st, [ch 3, skip next 3 sts, 1 sc in next st, ch 3, skip next 3 sts, 1 pc5 over round 7 sl st and into round 6 2-ch sp, ch 3, skip next 3 sts, 1 sc in next st] eight times, omit 1 sc on last rep, sl st in beginning sc (16 sc, 8 pc5, 24 x 3-ch sp).

Fasten off **yarn B**.

Round 9 (RS): using **yarn H**, in 3-ch sp between any 2 sc, ch 4 (counts as 1 tr), [2 tr, ch 3, 3 tr] in same sp, [ch 1, skip sc, 3 dc in next 3-ch sp, ch 1, skip pc5, 3 hdc in next 3-ch sp, ch 1, skip sc, 3 sc in next 3-ch sp, ch 1, skip sc, 3 hdc in next 3-ch sp, ch 1, skip pc5, 3 dc in next 3-ch sp, ch 1, skip sc, (3 tr, ch 3, 3 tr) in next 3-ch sp] four times, omit [3 tr, ch 3, 3 tr] on last rep, sl st in fourth ch of beginning ch 4 (84 sts, 24 x ch sp, 4 x 3-ch sp).

SKILL LEVEL

HOOK SIZE	BLOCK SIZE
US E/4 (3.5mm)	6 x 6in (15 x 15cm)

TECHNIQUES
Working over/into previous rounds/rows
(see page 119)

YARN/COLORS
Sample uses Scheepjes Softfun

A = Bumblebee (#2634)	E = Canary (#2518)
B = Snow (#2412)	F = Mint (#2640)
C = Rose (#2514)	G = Cool Blue (#2603)
D = Cantaloupe (#2652)	H = Orchid (#2657)

STITCHES
ch—chain

sl st—slip stitch

hdc—half double crochet

dc—double crochet

pc5—5 dc popcorn stitch (ch 1 to secure)

tr-3-cl—cluster made of treble crochet
3 sts together

fptr—front post treble crochet

MIX AND MATCH

Page 42 + Page 76

CHART KEY
For symbol key, see page 122

Round 10 (RS): sl st in each of next 2 sts, sl st in 3-ch sp, ch 2 (counts as 1 hdc), [1 hdc, ch 2, 2 hdc] in same sp, [(1 hdc in each of next 3 sts, 1 hdc in next ch sp) twice, 1 sc in each of next 4 sts, sl st in each of next 3 sts, 1 sc in each of next 4 sts, (1 hdc in each of next 3 sts, 1 hdc in next ch sp) twice, (2 hdc, ch 2, 2 hdc) in next 3-ch sp] four times, omit [2 hdc, ch 2, 2 hdc] on last rep, sl st in second ch of beginning ch 2 (124 sts). Fasten off **yarn H.**

Round 11 (RS): using **yarn C,** in any 2-ch sp, ch 1, [3 sc in 2-ch sp, 1 sc in each of next 31 sts] four times, sl st in beginning sc (136 sts). Fasten off **yarn C.**

Weave in ends and block.

HOOK SIZE	BLOCK SIZE
US C/2 (3mm)	6 x 6in (15 x 15cm)

TECHNIQUES

Working with multiple colors at the same time/
tapestry crochet (see page 121)

Changing color on row/round (see page 121)

YARN/COLORS

Sample uses Scheepjes Softfun

A = Latte (#2622)

B = Rose (#2514)

C = Candy Apple (#2410)

STITCHES

ch—chain

sl st—slip stitch

hdc—half double crochet

dc—double crochet

tr—treble crochet

MIX AND MATCH

Page 12 + Page 17 + Page 38

CHART KEY

For symbol key, see page 122

Scattered Hearts

A fun, contemporary block created with tapestry crochet.

Using **yarn A**, start with a magic ring.

Round 1 (RS): ch 3 (counts as 1 dc throughout), 11 dc into ring, sl st in third ch of beginning ch 3 (12 sts).

Round 2 (RS): sl st in sp between next 2 sts, [ch 3, 1 dc, ch 1, 2 dc] in same sp, skip next 2 sts; using **yarn B**, 3 dc in next st sp; using **yarn A**, [ch 1, 2 dc] in same sp, skip next 2 sts, 2 dc in next st sp, ch 1 (use this chain to change to **yarn B**); using **yarn B**, 3 dc in same sp, skip next 2 sts; using **yarn A**, [2 dc, ch 1, 2 dc] in next st sp, skip next 2 sts; using **yarn B**, 3 dc in next st sp; using **yarn A**, ch 1, 2 dc in same sp, skip next 2 sts, 2 dc in next st sp, ch 1 (use this chain to change to **yarn B**); using **yarn B**, 3 dc in same sp, skip next 2 sts; using **yarn A**, sl st in third ch of beginning ch 3 (28 sts).

Round 3 (RS): sl st in next st, sl st in next ch sp, [ch 3, 2 dc] in same sp, skip next 2 sts; [using **yarn B**, 3 dc in next st sp, skip next 3 sts, 3 dc in ch sp, skip next 2 sts; using **yarn A**, 3 dc in next st sp, skip next 2 sts; using **yarn B**, 3 dc in ch sp, skip next 3 sts, 3 dc in next st sp, skip next 2 sts; using **yarn A**, 3 dc in ch sp, skip

next 2 sts] twice, omit [yarn A, 3 dc in ch sp, skip next 2 sts] on last rep; using yarn A, sl st in third ch of beginning ch 3 (36 sts).

Fasten off yarn B.

Round 4 (RS): sl st in each of next 2 sts, sl st in next st sp, [ch 3, 3 dc] in same sp, skip next 3 sts, [4 dc in next st sp, skip next 3 sts] eleven times, sl st in third ch of beginning ch 3 (48 sts).

Round 5 (RS): sl st in next st, sl st in next st sp, [ch 3, 2 dc] in same sp, [skip next 2 sts, 3 dc in st sp, skip next 2 sts; using yarn C, 3 dc in st sp, skip next 2 sts; using yarn A, 3 dc in st sp] eight times, omit [yarn A, 3 dc in st sp] on last rep; using yarn A, sl st in third ch of beginning ch 3 (72 sts).

Do not fasten off.

Round 6 (RS): sl st in each of next 2 sts, sl st in next st sp, [ch 3, 2 dc] in same sp, skip next 3 sts; [(using yarn C, 3 dc in st sp, skip next 3 sts) twice; using yarn A, 3 dc in st sp, skip next 3 sts] eight times, omit [yarn A, 3 dc in st sp, skip next 3 sts] on last rep; using yarn A, sl st in third ch of beginning ch 3 (72 sts).

Fasten off yarn C.

Round 7 (RS): sl st in each of next 2 sts, sl st in next st sp, [ch 3, 2 dc] in same sp, [skip next 3 sts, (3 tr, ch 3, 3 tr) in st sp, skip next 3 sts, (3 dc in st sp, skip next 3 sts) twice, 3 hdc in st sp, (skip next 3 sts, 3 dc in st sp) twice] four times, omit final 3 dc on last rep, sl st in third ch of beginning ch 3 (84 sts).

Do not fasten off.

Round 8 (RS): sl st in each of next 5 sts, sl st in 3-ch sp, [ch 3, 2 dc, ch 2, 3 dc] in same sp, [skip next 3 sts, 3 dc in st sp, skip next 3 sts; using yarn B, 3 dc in st sp, skip next 3 sts; (using yarn A, 3 dc in st sp, skip next 3 sts) twice;

using yarn B, 3 dc in st sp, skip next 3 sts; using yarn A, 3 dc in st sp, skip next 3 sts, (3 dc, ch 2, 3 dc) in 2-ch sp] four times, omit [3 dc, ch 2, 3 dc] on last rep; using yarn A, sl st in third ch of beginning ch 3 (96 sts).

Do not fasten off.

Round 9 (RS): sl st in each of next 2 sts, sl st in 2-ch sp, [ch 3, 2 dc, ch 2, 3 dc] in same sp, [skip next 3 sts, 3 dc in st sp, skip next 3 sts; (using yarn B, 3 dc in st sp, skip next 3 sts) twice; using yarn A, 3 dc in st sp, skip next 3 sts; (using yarn B, 3 dc in st sp, skip next 3 sts) twice; using yarn A, 3 dc in st sp, skip next 3 sts, (3 dc, ch 2, 3 dc) in 2-ch sp] four times, omit [3 dc, ch 2, 3 dc] on last rep; using yarn

A, sl st in third ch of beginning ch 3 (108 sts).

Fasten off yarn B.

Round 10 (RS): sl st in each of next 2 sts, sl st in 2-ch sp, ch 1 (does not count as st) [[(3 hdc, ch 2, 3 hdc) in 2-ch sp, skip next 3 sts, (3 hdc in st sp, skip next 3 sts) eight times] four times, sl st in beginning hdc (120 sts).

Fasten off yarn A.

Weave in ends and block.

NOTE: From round 2 onward, you will need to switch between two shades at a time. One of these will always be yarn A. Do not fasten this off until instructed.

Single-color Granny Square

Perfect for beginners, you can also make this plain square in a rainbow of colors (see page 28).

Using **yarn A**, start with a magic ring.
Round 1 (WS): ch 3 (counts as 1 dc throughout), 2 dc into ring, ch 2, 3 dc into ring, ch 2, [3 dc, ch 2 into ring] twice, sl st in third ch of beginning ch 3, turn (12 sts).
Round 2 (RS): loosely sl st back in 2-ch sp, [ch 3, 2 dc] in same sp, [skip next 3 sts, (3 dc, ch 2, 3 dc) in 2-ch sp] three times, skip next 3 sts, 3 dc in 2-ch sp, ch 2, sl st in third ch of beginning ch 3, turn (24 sts).
Round 3 (WS): loosely sl st back in 2-ch sp, [ch 3, 2 dc] in same sp, [skip next 3 sts, 3 dc in st sp, skip next 3 sts, (3 dc, ch 2, 3 dc) in 2-ch sp] three times, skip next 3 sts, 3 dc in st sp, skip next 3 sts, 3 dc in 2-ch sp, ch 2, sl st in third ch of beginning ch 3, turn (36 sts).
Round 4 (RS): loosely sl st back in 2-ch sp, [ch 3, 2 dc] in same sp, [skip next 3 sts, (3 dc in st sp, skip next 3 sts) twice, (3 dc, ch 2, 3 dc) in 2-ch sp] three times, skip next 3 sts, [3 dc in st sp, skip next 3 sts] twice, 3 dc in 2-ch sp, ch 2, sl st in third ch of beginning ch 3, turn (48 sts).
Round 5 (WS): loosely sl st back in 2-ch sp, [ch 3, 2 dc] in same sp, [skip next 3 sts, (3 dc in st sp, skip next 3 sts) three times, (3 dc, ch 2,

SKILL LEVEL
◉ ◉ ◉

HOOK SIZE	BLOCK SIZE
US G/6 (4mm)	6 x 6in (15 x 15cm)

YARN/COLORS
Sample uses Scheepjes Softfun
A = Hot Pink (#2495)

STITCHES
ch—chain
sl st—slip stitch
dc—double crochet

MIX AND MATCH

Page 25 ✚ Page 46 ✚ Page 99

CHART KEY
For symbol key, see page 122

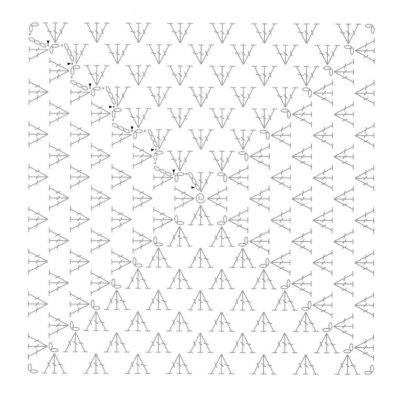

3 dc) in 2-ch sp] three times, skip next 3 sts, [3 dc in st sp, skip next 3 sts] three times, 3 dc in 2-ch sp, ch 2, sl st in third ch of beginning ch 3, turn (60 sts).

Round 6 (RS): loosely sl st back in 2-ch sp, [ch 3, 2 dc] in same sp, [skip next 3 sts, (3 dc in st sp, skip next 3 sts) four times, (3 dc, ch 2, 3 dc) in 2-ch sp] three times, skip next 3 sts, [3 dc in st sp, skip next 3 sts] four times, 3 dc in 2-ch sp, ch 2, sl st in third ch of beginning ch 3, turn (72 sts).

Round 7 (WS): loosely sl st back in 2-ch sp, [ch 3, 2 dc] in same sp, [skip next 3 sts, (3 dc

in st sp, skip next 3 sts) five times, (3 dc, ch 2, 3 dc) in 2-ch sp] three times, skip next 3 sts, [3 dc in st sp, skip next 3 sts] five times, 3 dc in 2-ch sp, ch 2, sl st in third ch of beginning ch 3, turn (84 sts).

Round 8 (RS): loosely sl st back in 2-ch sp, [ch 3, 2 dc] in same sp, [skip next 3 sts, (3 dc in st sp, skip next 3 sts) six times, (3 dc, ch 2, 3 dc) in 2-ch sp] three times, skip next 3 sts, [3 dc in st sp, skip next 3 sts] six times, 3 dc in 2-ch sp, ch 2, sl st in third ch of beginning ch 3 (96 sts).

Fasten off **yarn A**.

Weave in ends and block.

NOTES: The majority of this square is worked in the spaces between stitches. Do not work directly into a stitch unless otherwise instructed.

A flat square is achieved by alternating the sides each round is worked on: odd rounds are worked on WS; even rounds are worked on RS.

Two-color Intarsia Square

A twist on the classic granny square with endless color combination possibilities.

Using **yarn A**, start with a magic ring.

Round 1 (WS): ch 3 (counts as 1 dc throughout), 2 dc into ring, ch 2, 3 dc into ring, ch 1; using **yarn B** (join/change of color to be counted as ch 1 throughout), [3 dc, ch 2 into ring] twice, sl st in third ch of beginning ch 3, turn (12 sts).

Round 2 (RS): using **yarn B**, loosely sl st back in 2-ch sp, [ch 3, 2 dc] in same sp, skip next 3 sts, [3 dc, ch 2, 3 dc] in 2-ch sp, skip next 3 sts, 3 dc in 2-ch sp, ch 1; using **yarn A**, 3 dc in same sp, skip next 3 sts, [3 dc, ch 2, 3 dc] in 2-ch sp, skip next 3 sts, 3 dc in 2-ch sp, ch 2, sl st in third ch of beginning ch 3, turn (24 sts).

Round 3 (WS): using **yarn A**, loosely sl st back in 2-ch sp, [ch 3, 2 dc] in same sp, skip next 3 sts, 3 dc in st sp, skip next 3 sts, [3 dc, ch 2, 3 dc] in 2-ch sp, skip next 3 sts, 3 dc in st sp, skip next 3 sts, 3 dc in 2-ch sp, ch 1; using **yarn B**, 3 dc in same sp, skip next 3 sts, 3 dc in st sp, skip next 3 sts, [3 dc, ch 2, 3 dc] in 2-ch sp, skip next 3 sts, 3 dc in st sp, skip next 3 sts, 3 dc in 2-ch sp, ch 2, sl st in third ch of beginning ch 3, turn (36 sts).

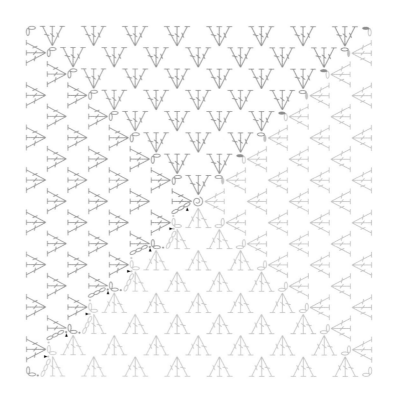

Round 4 (RS): using **yarn B**, loosely sl st back in 2-ch sp, [ch 3, 2 dc] in same sp, skip next 3 sts, [3 dc in st sp, skip next 3 sts] twice, [3 dc, ch 2, 3 dc] in 2-ch sp, skip next 3 sts, [3 dc in st sp, skip next 3 sts] twice, 3 dc in 2-ch sp, ch 1; using **yarn A**, 3 dc in same sp, skip next 3 sts, [3 dc in st sp, skip next 3 sts] twice, [3 dc, ch 2, 3 dc] in 2-ch sp, skip next 3 sts, [3 dc in st sp, skip next 3 sts] twice, 3 dc in 2-ch sp, ch 2, sl st in third ch of beginning ch 3, turn (48 sts).

Round 5 (WS): using **yarn A**, loosely sl st back in 2-ch sp, [ch 3, 2 dc] in same sp, skip next 3 sts, [3 dc in st sp, skip next 3 sts] three times, [3 dc, ch 2, 3 dc] in 2-ch sp, skip next 3 sts, [3 dc in st sp, skip next 3 sts] three times, 3 dc in 2-ch sp, ch 1; using **yarn B**, 3 dc in same sp, skip next 3 sts, [3 dc in st sp, skip next 3 sts] three times, [3 dc, ch 2, 3 dc] in 2-ch sp, skip next 3 sts, [3 dc in st sp, skip next 3 sts] three times, 3 dc in 2-ch sp, ch 2, sl st in third ch of beginning ch 3, turn (60 sts).

Round 6 (RS): using **yarn B**, loosely sl st back in 2-ch sp, [ch 3, 2 dc] in same sp, skip next 3 sts, [3 dc in st sp, skip next 3 sts] four times, [3 dc, ch 2, 3 dc] in 2-ch sp, skip next 3 sts, [3 dc in st sp, skip next 3 sts] four times, 3 dc in 2-ch sp, ch 1; using **yarn A**, 3 dc in same sp, skip next 3 sts, [3 dc in st sp, skip next 3 sts] four times, [3 dc, ch 2, 3 dc] in 2-ch sp, skip next 3 sts, [3 dc in st sp, skip next 3 sts] four times, 3 dc in 2-ch sp, ch 2, sl st in third ch of beginning ch 3, turn (72 sts).

Round 7 (WS): using **yarn A**, loosely sl st back in 2-ch sp, [ch 3, 2 dc] in same sp, skip next 3 sts, [3 dc in st sp, skip next 3 sts] five times, [3 dc, ch 2, 3 dc] in 2-ch sp, skip next 3 sts, [3 dc in st sp, skip next 3 sts] five times,

3 dc in 2-ch sp, ch 1; using **yarn B**, 3 dc in same sp, skip next 3 sts, [3 dc in st sp, skip next 3 sts] five times, [3 dc, ch 2, 3 dc] in 2-ch sp, skip next 3 sts, [3 dc in st sp, skip next 3 sts] five times, 3 dc in 2-ch sp, ch 2, sl st in third ch of beginning ch 3, turn (84 sts).

Round 8 (RS): using **yarn B**, loosely sl st back in 2-ch sp, [ch 3, 2 dc] in same sp, skip next 3 sts, [3 dc in st sp, skip next 3 sts] six times, [3 dc, ch 2, 3 dc] in 2-ch sp, skip next 3 sts, [3 dc in st sp, skip next 3 sts] six times, 3 dc in 2-ch sp, ch 1; using **yarn A**, 3 dc in same sp, skip next 3 sts, [3 dc in st sp, skip next 3 sts] six times, [3 dc, ch 2, 3 dc] in 2-ch sp, skip next 3 sts, [3 dc in st sp, skip next 3 sts] six times,

3 dc in 2-ch sp, ch 2, sl st in third ch of beginning ch 3 (96 sts).
Fasten off **yarn A** and **yarn B**.

Weave in ends and block.

NOTES: Do not fasten off any colors until instructed.
The majority of this square is worked in the spaces between stitches. Do not work directly into a stitch unless instructed.
A flat square is achieved by alternating the sides each round is worked on: odd rounds are worked on WS; even rounds are worked on RS.

Colorblock Double Crochet Square

An easy essential to have in your crochet pattern collection.

———

Using **yarn A**, start with a magic ring.

Round 1 (WS): ch 3 (counts as 1 dc throughout), 2 dc into ring, ch 2, 3 dc into ring, ch 1; using **yarn B** (join/change of color to be counted as ch 1 throughout), [3 dc, ch 2 into ring] twice, sl st in third ch of beginning ch 3, turn (12 sts).

Round 2 (RS): using **yarn B**, loosely sl st back in 2-ch sp, [ch 3, 1 dc] in same sp, 1 dc in each st until next 2-ch sp, [2 dc, ch 2, 2 dc] in 2-ch sp, 1 dc in each st until next 2-ch sp, 2 dc in 2-ch sp, ch 1; using **yarn A**, 2 dc in same sp, 1 dc in each st until next 2-ch sp, [2 dc, ch 2, 2 dc] in 2-ch sp, 1 dc in each st until next 2-ch sp, 2 dc in 2-ch sp, ch 2, sl st in third ch of beginning ch 3, turn (28 sts).

Round 3 (WS): using **yarn A**, loosely sl st back in 2-ch sp, [ch 3, 1 dc] in same sp, 1 dc in each st until next 2-ch sp, [2 dc, ch 2, 2 dc] in 2-ch sp, 1 dc in each st until next 2-ch sp, 2 dc in 2-ch sp, ch 1; using **yarn B**, 2 dc in same sp, 1 dc in each st until next 2-ch sp, [2 dc, ch 2, 2 dc] in 2-ch sp, 1 dc in each st until next 2-ch sp, 2 dc in 2-ch sp, ch 2, sl st in third ch of beginning ch 3, turn (44 sts).

Round 4 (RS): rep round 2 (60 sts).

Round 5 (WS): rep round 3 (76 sts).

Round 6 (RS): rep round 2 (92 sts).

Round 7 (WS): rep round 3 (108 sts).

Round 8 (RS): rep round 2 (124 sts).

Fasten off **yarn A** and **yarn B**.

Weave in ends and block.

NOTES: This square requires you to work with two different colors of yarn within a single round using a method called intarsia. Do not fasten off any colors until instructed. A flat square is achieved by alternating the sides each round is worked on: odd rounds are worked on WS; even rounds are worked on RS.

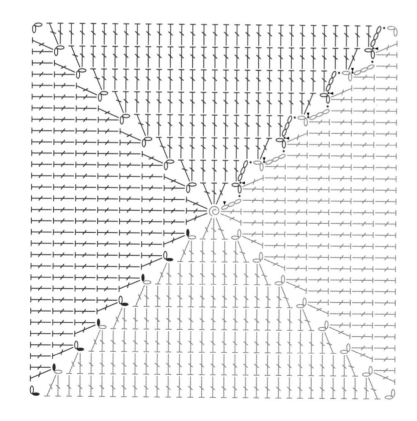

SKILL LEVEL

HOOK SIZE	BLOCK SIZE
US E/4 (3.5mm)	6 x 6in (15 x 15cm)

TECHNIQUES

Working with multiple colors at the same time/
intarsia crochet (see page 121)

Changing color on row/round (see page 121)

YARN/COLORS

Sample uses Scheepjes Softfun

A = Cool Blue (#2603)

B = Dark Turquoise (#2511)

STITCHES

ch—chain

sl st—slip stitch

dc—double crochet

MIX AND MATCH

  +   +

Page 58 + Page 78 + Page 66

CHART KEY

For symbol key, see page 122

HOOK SIZE	BLOCK SIZE
US E/4 (3.5mm)	6 x 6in (15 x 15cm)

YARN/COLORS
Sample uses Scheepjes Softfun

A = Deep Violet (#2515)

B = Dark Turquoise (#2511)

C = Botanical (#2615)

D = Apple (#2516)

E = Butterscotch (#2610)

F = Tangerine (#2427)

G = Candy Apple (#2410)

H = Hot Pink (#2495)

I = Rose (#2514)

J = Light Rose (#2513)

K = Snow (#2412)

STITCHES
ch—chain

sl st—slip stitch

sc—single crochet

hdc—half double crochet

dc—double crochet

tr—treble crochet

MIX AND MATCH

Page 38 ➕ Page 12

CHART KEY
For symbol key, see page 122

60s Floral Motif
A riot of color, multiple squares would make a lovely pillow.

Using **yarn A**, start with a magic ring.

Round 1 (WS): ch 1 (does not count as st), 8 sc into ring, sl st in beginning sc, turn (8 sts).

Round 2 (RS): ch 3 (counts as 1 sl st, ch 2), [sl st in next st, ch 2] seven times, sl st in first ch of beginning ch 3 (8 x 2-ch sp).

Fasten off **yarn A**.

Round 3 (RS): using **yarn B**, [1 sl st, ch 2, 2 hdc] in each 2-ch sp around, sl st in beginning sl st, turn (8 x hdc blocks).

Fasten off **yarn B**.

Round 4 (WS): using **yarn C**, rep round 3.

Fasten off **yarn C**.

Round 5 (RS): using **yarn D**, [1 sl st, ch 3, 3 dc] in each 2-ch sp around, sl st in beginning sl st, turn (8 x dc blocks).

Fasten off **yarn D**.

Round 6 (WS): using **yarn E**, [1 sl st, ch 4, 4 tr] in each 3-ch sp around, sl st in beginning sl st, turn (8 x tr blocks).

Fasten off **yarn E**.

Round 7 (RS): using yarn F, [[(1 sl st, ch 3, 3 dc) in 4-ch sp, skip next sl st, skip next st, (1 sl st, ch 3, 3 dc) in next st, skip next 2 sts] eight times, sl st in beginning sl st, turn (16 x dc blocks).

Fasten off yarn F.

Round 8 (WS): using yarn G, [1 sl st, ch 3, 3 dc] in any 3-ch sp, [1 sl st, ch 3, 3 dc] in each of next three 3-ch sp, ch 5, [(1 sl st, ch 3, 3 dc) in each of next four 3-ch sp, ch 5] three times, sl st in beginning sl st, turn (16 x dc blocks, 4 x 5-ch sp).

Fasten off yarn G.

Round 9 (RS): using yarn H, in any 5-ch sp, ch 1 (does not count as st), [1 sc in 5-ch sp, ch 7, (1 sl st, ch 3, 3 dc) in each of next three 3-ch sp, sl st in next 3-ch sp, ch 7] four times, sl st in beginning sc (12 x dc blocks, 8 x 7-ch sp, 4 sc).

Fasten off yarn H.

Round 10 (RS): using yarn I, in any sc, ch 7 (counts as 1 tr, ch 3), 1 tr in same st, [ch 3, 1 sc in 7-ch sp, ch 3, skip sl st, (skip 3-ch sp, 1 sc in next st, 1 hdc in each of next 2 sts, 1 dc in sl st) three times, ch 3, 1 sc in 7-ch sp, ch 3, (1 tr, ch 3, 1 tr) in sc] four times, omit [1 tr, ch 3, 1 tr] on last rep, sl st in fourth ch of beginning ch 7 (64 sts, 20 x 3-ch sp).

Fasten off yarn I.

Round 11 (RS): using yarn J, in any corner 3-ch sp, ch 2 (does not count as st), [[(2 hdc, ch 1, 2 hdc) in corner 3-ch sp, skip tr, 3 sc in next 3-ch sp, skip sc, 2 sc in next 3-ch sp, sl st in each of next 12 sts, 2 sc in 3-ch sp, skip

sc, 3 sc in next 3-ch sp, skip tr] four times, sl st in beginning sc (104 sts).

Fasten off yarn J.

Round 12 (RS): using yarn K, in any ch sp, ch 1 (does not count as st), [[(1 sc, ch 1, 1 sc) in ch sp, 1 sc in each of next 26 sts] four times, sl st in beginning sc (112 sts).

Fasten off yarn K.

Weave in ends and block.

NOTE: Take note of which side each round is made on.

Houndstooth Pattern

Crochet the timeless monochrome fashion print that never goes out of style.

Using **yarn A**, ch 25.

Row 1 (RS): 1 sc in second ch from hook, 1 dc in next ch, [1 sc in next ch, 1 dc in next ch] eleven times, join **yarn B**, turn (24 sts).
Fasten off **yarn A**.

Row 2 (WS): ch 1 (does not count as st throughout), 1 sc in same st, 1 dc in next st, [1 sc in next ch, 1 dc in next ch] eleven times, join **yarn A**, turn (24 sts).
Fasten off **yarn B**.

Row 3 (RS): ch 1, 1 sc in same st, 1 dc in next st, [1 sc in next ch, 1 dc in next ch] eleven times, join **yarn B**, turn (24 sts).
Fasten off **yarn A**.

Rows 4–19: rep rows 2 and 3 eight times, omit join **yarn B** at end of row 19.
Fasten off **yarn A**.

BORDER

To achieve a border that is as neat as possible, (RS): using **yarn A**, evenly space 26 sl st along one of the vertical edges of work, fasten off, and repeat on the opposite side.
Fasten off **yarn A**.

Round 1 (RS): using **yarn A**, in last st of row 19, ch 1, 2 sc in same st, [ch 1, 1 sc in each of next 26 sl st, ch 1, 2 sc in next st, 1 sc in each of next 22 sts, 2 sc in next st] twice, omit second 2 sc on last rep, sl st in beginning sc (104 sts).
Fasten off **yarn A**.

Round 2 (RS): using **yarn C**, in any 2-ch sp, ch 2 (does not count as st), [(1 hdc, ch 2, 1 hdc) in ch sp, 1 hdc in each of next 26 sts] four times, sl st in beginning hdc (112 sts).
Fasten off **yarn C**.

Weave in ends and block.

NOTE: The square is worked back and forth in rows with an edging worked in rounds.

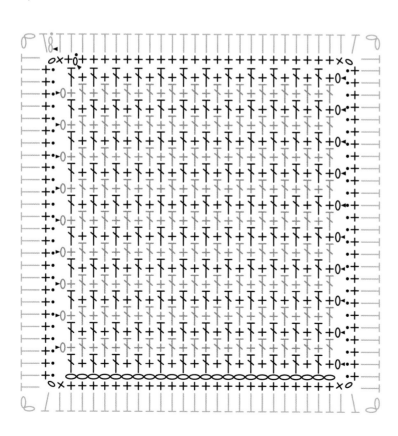

HOOK SIZE	BLOCK SIZE
US G/6 (4mm)	6 x 6in (15 x 15cm)

TECHNIQUES

Changing color on row/round (see page 121)

Working into round/row ends (see page 125)

YARN/COLORS

Sample uses Scheepjes Softfun

A = Charcoal (#2628)

B = Snow (#2412)

C = Botanical (#2615)

STITCHES

ch—chain

sl st—slip stitch

sc—single crochet

hdc—half double crochet

dc—double crochet

MIX AND MATCH

Page 20   +   Page 32

CHART KEY

For symbol key, see page 122

HOOK SIZE	BLOCK SIZE
US E/4 (3.5mm)	6 x 6in (15 x 15cm)

TECHNIQUES

Changing color on row/round (see page 121)
Working into round/row ends (see page 125)

YARN/COLORS

Sample uses Scheepjes Softfun
A = Butterscotch (#2610)
B = Rose (#2514)
C = Light Rose (#2513)
D = Botanical (#2615)
E = Orchid (#2657)
F = Snow (#2412)

STITCHES

ch—chain
sl st—slip stitch
sc—single crochet
dc—double crochet

MIX AND MATCH

Page 34 ➕ Page 30

CHART KEY

For symbol key, see page 122

Peaches and Cream

This square uses color and stitches for a striped effect.

Using **yarn A**, start with a magic ring.
Round 1 (RS): ch 3 (counts as 1 dc throughout), 2 dc into ring, ch 2, [3 dc, ch 2 into ring] three times, sl st in third ch of beginning ch 3 (12 sts).
Fasten off **yarn A**.
Round 2 (RS): using **yarn B**, in any 2-ch sp, [ch 3, 2 dc, ch 2, 3 dc] in same sp, [skip next 3 sts, (3 dc, ch 2, 3 dc) in next 2-ch sp] three times, sl st in third ch of beginning ch 3 (24 sts).
Fasten off **yarn B**.

Round 3 (RS): using **yarn C**, in any 2-ch sp, [ch 3, 2 dc, ch 2, 3 dc] in same sp, [skip next 3 sts, 3 dc in next st sp, skip next 3 sts (3 dc, ch 2, 3 dc) in next 2-ch sp] four times, omit [3 dc, ch 2, 3 dc] on last rep, sl st in third ch of beginning ch 3 (36 sts).
Fasten off **yarn C**.
Round 4 (RS): using **yarn D**, in any 2-ch sp, [ch 3, 2 dc, ch 2, 3 dc] in same sp, [skip next 3 sts, (3 dc in next st sp, skip next 3 sts) twice, (3 dc, ch 2, 3 dc) in next 2-ch sp] four times, omit [3 dc, ch 2, 3 dc] on last rep, sl st in third

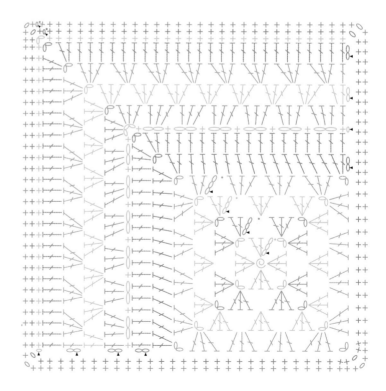

ch of beginning ch 3 (48 sts).

Fasten off **yarn D**.

Row 5 (RS): using **yarn E**, in any 2-ch sp, ch 2 (does not count as st throughout), 2 dc in same sp, 1 dc in each of next 12 sts, [2 dc, ch 2, 2 dc] in 2-ch sp, 1 dc in each of next 12 sts, 2 dc in 2-ch sp, join **yarn F**, turn (32 sts).

Fasten off **yarn E**.

Row 6 (WS): ch 2, 1 dc in each st until next 2-ch sp, [2 dc, ch 2, 2 dc] in 2-ch sp, 1 dc in each st until end, join **yarn A**, turn (36 sts).

Fasten off **yarn F**.

Row 7 (RS): ch 1 (does not count as st throughout), 1 sc in same st, ch 2, skip next 2 sts, [1 sc in next st, ch 2, skip next 2 sts] five times, [1 sc, ch 3, 1 sc] in next 2-ch sp, [ch 2, skip next 2 sts, 1 sc in next st] six times, join **yarn B**, turn (14 sc, 12 x 2-ch sp, 1 x 3-ch sp).

Fasten off **yarn A**.

Row 8 (WS): ch 2, 1 dc in same st, [3 dc in 2-ch sp, skip next st] six times, [3 dc, ch 2, 3 dc] in 3-ch sp, [skip next st, 3 dc in 2-ch sp] six times, 1 dc in last st, join **yarn C**, turn (44 sts).

Fasten off **yarn B**.

Row 9 (RS): ch 2, 1 dc in same st, 1 dc in next st sp, skip next 3 sts, [3 dc in next st sp, skip next 3 sts] six times, [3 dc, ch 2, 3 dc] in 2-ch sp, skip next 3 sts, [3 dc in next st sp, skip next 3 sts] six times, 1 dc in next st sp, 1 dc in last st, join **yarn D**, turn (46 sts).

Fasten off **yarn C**.

Row 10 (WS): ch 2, 1 dc in same st, skip next st, [3 dc in next st sp, skip next 3 sts] seven times, [3 dc, ch 2, 3 dc] in 2-ch sp, [skip next 3 sts, 3 dc in next st sp] seven times, skip next st, 1 dc in last st, join **yarn F**, turn (50 sts).

Fasten off **yarn D**.

Row 11 (RS): rep row 6, join **yarn A**, turn (54 sts).

Fasten off **yarn F**.

Row 12 (WS): ch 1, 1 sc in each of next 27 sts, [1 sc, ch 2, 1 sc] in 2-ch sp, 1 sc in each of next 27 sts, turn (56 sts).

Fasten off **yarn A**.

BORDER

Round 13 (RS): using **yarn E**, in 2-ch sp (row 12), ch 1, [1 sc, ch 1, 1 sc] in same sp, 1 sc in each of next 28 sts, ch 1, evenly space 27 sc until you reach next 2-ch sp, [2 sc, ch 1, 2 sc] in 2-ch sp, 1 sc in each of next 12 sts, evenly space 15 sc along remainder of side, ch 1,

1 sc in each of next 28 sts, sl st in beginning sc (116 sts).

Fasten off **yarn E**.

Round 14 (RS): using **yarn B**, in any ch sp, ch 1 (does not count as st), [[1 sc, ch 1, 1 sc] in ch sp, 1 sc in each of next 29 sts] four times, sl st in beginning sc (124 sts).

Fasten off **yarn B**.

Weave in ends and block.

NOTE: The square is worked from bottom corner, then back and forth in rows, with an edging worked in rounds.

HOOK SIZE	BLOCK SIZE
US E/4 (3.5mm)	6 x 6in (15 x 15cm)

TECHNIQUES
Changing color on row/round (see page 121)
Working into round/row ends (see page 125)

YARN/COLORS
Sample uses Scheepjes Softfun
A = Rose (#2514)
B = Orchid (#2657)
C = Cool Blue (#2603)
D = Mint (#2640)
E = Canary (#2518)
F = Cantaloupe (#2652)
G = Snow (#2412)

STITCHES
ch—chain
sl st—slip stitch
sc—single crochet
hdc —half double crochet
dc—double crochet

MIX AND MATCH

Page 32 **+** Page 40

CHART KEY
For symbol key, see page 122

Sorbet Square
A really simple square that shows off fresh, juicy colors.

Using yarn A, ch 4.
Row 1 (RS): 4 dc in fourth ch from hook, join yarn B, turn (5 sts).
Fasten off yarn A.
Row 2 (WS): ch 3 (counts as 1 dc throughout), 3 dc in next st sp, skip next 3 sts, 4 dc in next st sp, turn (8 sts).
Row 3 (RS): ch 3, [3 dc in next st sp, skip next 3 sts] twice, 4 dc in next st sp, join yarn C, turn (11 sts).

Fasten off yarn B.
Row 4 (WS): ch 3, [3 dc in next st sp, skip next 3 sts] three times, 4 dc in next st sp, join yarn B, turn (14 sts).
Fasten off yarn C.
Row 5 (RS): ch 3, [3 dc in next st sp, skip next 3 sts] four times, 4 dc in next st sp, join yarn C, turn (17 sts).
Fasten off yarn B.
Row 6 (WS): ch 3, [3 dc in next st sp, skip next

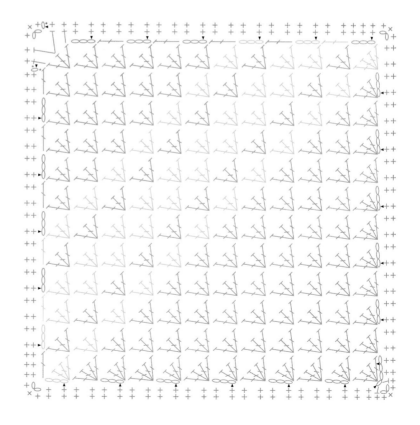

3 sts] five times, 4 dc in next st sp, turn (20 sts).

Row 7 (RS): ch 3, [3 dc in next st sp, skip next 3 sts] six times, 4 dc in next st sp, join **yarn D**, turn (23 sts).

Fasten off **yarn C**.

Row 8 (WS): ch 3, [3 dc in next st sp, skip next 3 sts] seven times, 4 dc in next st sp, join **yarn C**, turn (26 sts).

Fasten off **yarn D**.

Row 9 (RS): ch 3, [3 dc in next st sp, skip next 3 sts] eight times, 4 dc in next st sp, join **yarn D**, turn (29 sts).

Fasten off **yarn C**.

Row 10 (WS): ch 3, [3 dc in next st sp, skip next 3 sts] nine times, 4 dc in next st sp, turn (32 sts).

Row 11 (RS): ch 3, [3 dc in next st sp, skip next 3 sts] ten times, 4 dc in next st sp, join **yarn E**, turn (35 sts).

Fasten off **yarn D**.

Row 12 (WS): ch 3, [3 dc in next st sp, skip next 3 sts] eleven times, 4 dc in next st sp, join **yarn D**, turn (38 sts).

Fasten off **yarn E**.

Row 13 (RS): ch 3, skip next 3 sts, [3 dc in next st sp, skip next 3 sts] eleven times, 1 dc in next st sp, join **yarn E**, turn (35 sts).

Fasten off **yarn D**.

Row 14 (WS): ch 3, skip next 3 sts, [3 dc in next st sp, skip next 3 sts] ten times, 1 dc in next st sp, turn (32 sts).

Row 15 (RS): ch 3, skip next 3 sts, [3 dc in next st sp, skip next 3 sts] nine times, 1 dc in next st sp, join **yarn F**, turn (29 sts).

Fasten off **yarn E**.

Row 16 (WS): ch 3, skip next 3 sts, [3 dc in next st sp, skip next 3 sts] eight times, 1 dc in next st sp, join **yarn E**, turn (26 sts).

Fasten off **yarn F**.

Row 17 (RS): ch 3, skip next 3 sts, [3 dc in next st sp, skip next 3 sts] seven times, 1 dc in next st sp, join **yarn F**, turn (23 sts).

Fasten off **yarn E**.

Row 18 (WS): ch 3, skip next 3 sts, [3 dc in next st sp, skip next 3 sts] six times, 1 dc in next st sp, turn (20 sts).

Row 19 (RS): ch 3, skip next 3 sts, [3 dc in next st sp, skip next 3 sts] five times, 1 dc in next st sp, join **yarn A**, turn (17 sts).

Fasten off **yarn F**.

Row 20 (WS): ch 3, skip next 3 sts, [3 dc in next st sp, skip next 3 sts] four times, 1 dc in next st sp, join **yarn F**, turn (14 sts).

Fasten off **yarn A**.

Row 21 (RS): ch 3, skip next 3 sts, [3 dc in next st sp, skip next 3 sts] three times, 1 dc in next st sp, join **yarn A**, turn (11 sts).

Fasten off **yarn F**.

Row 22 (WS): ch 3, skip next 3 sts, [3 dc in next st sp, skip next 3 sts] twice, 1 dc in next st sp, turn (8 sts).

Row 23 (RS): ch 3, skip next 3 sts, 3 dc in next st sp, skip next 3 sts, 1 dc in next st sp (5 sts).

Do not fasten off **yarn A**.

BORDER

Round 1 (RS): using **yarn A**, sl st in side of last dc made in row 23, ch 1 (does not count as st), 2 sc in side of same st, [2 sc in next 3-ch sp, 2 sc in side of next dc] four times, 2 sc in next 3-ch sp, 3 sc in side of next dc, ch 2, [2 sc in next 3-ch sp, 2 sc in side of next dc] six times, [1 hdc, ch 2, 1 hdc] in corner ch (this will be the same ch as 4 dc from row 1 were made in), [2 sc in next 3-ch sp, 2 sc in side of next dc] six times, ch 2, 3 sc in next 3-ch sp, [2 sc in side of next dc, 2 sc in next 3-ch sp] five times, 1 sc in next st, [1 hdc, ch 2, 1 hdc] in next st, 1 sc in next st, sl st in beginning sc (100 sts).

Fasten off **yarn A**.

Round 2 (RS): using **yarn G**, in any 2-ch sp, ch 1 (does not count as st), [3 sc in 2-ch sp, 1 sc in each of next 25 sts] four times, sl st in beginning sc (112 sts).

Fasten off **yarn G**.

Weave in ends and block.

NOTE: The majority of this square is worked in the spaces between stitches. Do not work directly into a stitch unless otherwise instructed.

Diamond Daze

Try making this square for a more challenging project.

MAIN BODY

Using yarn A, ch 6.

Round 1 (RS): 1 dc in third ch from hook, 1 dc in each of next 3 ch (4 sts/1 block).

Fasten off **yarn A**.

Round 2 (RS): using **yarn B**, in first dc of round 1, ch 2 (does not count as st throughout), 1 dc in same st, [1 dc in each of next 2 sts, (1 dc, ch 2, 1 sl st) in next st, ch 4, 1 dc in third ch from hook, 1 dc in remaining ch, (1 sl st, ch 2, 1 dc) in next st] twice, omit [1 sl st, ch 2, 1 dc] on last rep, sl st in first st of round 2 (4 blocks).

Fasten off **yarn B**.

Round 3 (RS): using **yarn C**, in first dc of round 2, ch 2, 1 dc in same st, 1 dc next st, [(1 dc in next st, {1 dc, ch 2, 1 sl st} in next st) twice, ch 4, 1 dc in third ch from hook, 1 dc in remaining ch, (1 sl st, ch 2, 1 dc) in next st, 1 dc in next st] twice, sl st in first st of round 3 (8 blocks).

Fasten off **yarn C**.

SKILL LEVEL

HOOK SIZE	BLOCK SIZE
US C/2 (3mm)	6 x 6in (15 x 15cm)

TECHNIQUES
Working over/into previous rounds/rows (see page 119)

YARN/COLORS
Sample uses Scheepjes Softfun
A = Bumblebee (#2634)
B = Snow (#2412)
C = Light Rose (#2513)
D = Rose (#2514)
E = Botanical (#2615)
F = Denim (#2489)

STITCHES
ch—chain
sl st—slip stitch
sc—single crochet
hdc—half double crochet
dc—double crochet

MIX AND MATCH

Page 80 + Page 46

CHART KEY
For symbol key, see page 122

Corner 3

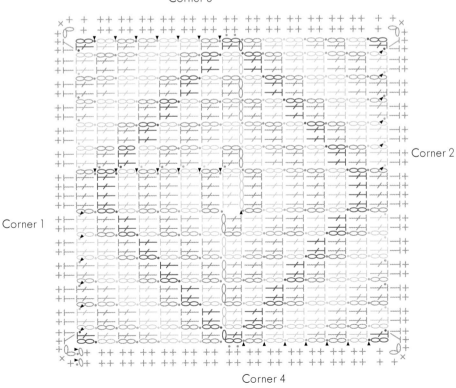

Corner 1

Corner 2

Corner 4

Round 4 (RS): using yarn D, in first dc of round 3, ch 2, 1 dc in same st, 1 dc next st, [(1 dc in next st, {1 dc, ch 2, 1 sl st} in next st) three times, ch 4, 1 dc in third ch from hook, 1 dc in remaining ch, ({1 sl st, ch 2, 1 dc} in next st, 1 dc in next st) three times] twice, omit [(1 sl st, ch 2, 1 dc) in next st, 1 dc in next st] on last rep, sl st in first st of round 4 (12 blocks).

Fasten off yarn D.

Round 5 (RS): using yarn B, in first dc of round 4, ch 2, 1 dc in same st, 1 dc next st, [(1 dc in next st, {1 dc, ch 2, 1 sl st} in next st) four times, ch 4, 1 dc in third ch from hook, 1 dc in remaining ch, ({1 sl st, ch 2, 1 dc} in next st, 1 dc in next st) four times] twice, omit [(1 sl st, ch 2, 1 dc) in next st, 1 dc in next st] on last rep, sl st in first st of round 5 (16 blocks).

Fasten off yarn B.

Round 6 (RS): using yarn E, in first dc of round 5, ch 2, 1 dc in same st, 1 dc next st, [(1 dc in next st, {1 dc, ch 2, 1 sl st} in next st) five times, ch 4, 1 dc in third ch from hook, 1 dc in remaining ch, ({1 sl st, ch 2, 1 dc} in next st, 1 dc in next st) five times] twice, omit [(1 sl st, ch 2, 1 dc) in next st, 1 dc in next st] on last rep, sl st in first st of round 6 (20 blocks).

Fasten off yarn E.

Round 7 (RS): using yarn F, in first dc of round 6, ch 2, 1 dc in same st, 1 dc next st, [(1 dc in next st, {1 dc, ch 2, 1 sl st} in next st) six times, ch 3, 1 dc in third ch from hook, ({1 sl st, ch 2, 1 dc} in next st, 1 dc in next st) six times] twice, omit [(1 sl st, ch 2, 1 dc) in next st, 1 dc in next st] on last rep, sl st in first st of round 7 (24 blocks).

Fasten off yarn F.

Round 8 (RS): using yarn B, in first dc of round 7, ch 2, 1 dc in same st, 1 dc next st, [(1 dc in next st, {1 dc, ch 2, 1 sl st} in next st) six times, (1 dc, ch 2, 1 sl st) in next st, 2 sl st in next 2-ch sp, (1 sl st, ch 2, 1 dc) in next st, ({1 sl st, ch 2, 1 dc} in next st, 1 dc in next st) six times] twice, omit [(1 sl st, ch 2, 1 dc) in next st, 1 dc in next st] on last rep, sl st in first st of round 8 (26 blocks).

Fasten off yarn B.

CORNERS

Corner 1:

Row 1 (RS): using **yarn A**, sl st in second 2-ch sp made in round 8, [1 dc in next st, (1 dc, ch 2, 1 sl st) in next st] five times, 1 dc in next st, ch 2, sl st in next 2-ch sp (6 blocks).

Fasten off **yarn A**.

Row 2 (RS): using **yarn C**, sl st in first 2-ch sp of row 1, ch 2, [1 dc in next st, (1 sl st, ch 2, 1 dc) in next st] four times, 1 dc in next st, sl st in next 2-ch sp (5 blocks).

Fasten off **yarn C**.

Row 3 (RS): using **yarn D**, sl st in first 2-ch sp of row 2, ch 2, [1 dc in next st, (1 sl st, ch 2, 1 dc) in next st] three times, 1 dc in next st, sl st in next 2-ch sp (4 blocks).

Fasten off **yarn D**.

Row 4 (RS): using **yarn B,** sl st in first 2-ch sp of row 3, ch 2, [1 dc in next st, (1 sl st, ch 2, 1 dc) in next st] twice, 1 dc in next st, sl st in next 2-ch sp (3 blocks).

Fasten off **yarn B**.

Row 5 (RS): using **yarn E**, sl st in first 2-ch sp of row 4, ch 2, 1 dc in next st, [1 sl st, ch 2, 1 dc] in next st, 1 dc in next st, sl st in next 2-ch sp (2 blocks).

Fasten off **yarn E**.

Row 6 (RS): using **yarn F**, sl st in first 2-ch sp of row 5, ch 2, 1 dc in next st, sl st in next 2-ch sp (1 block).

Fasten off **yarn F**.

Corner 2: rep instructions as per corner 1, starting in 2-ch sp to the left of the other 4 dc side of diamond.

Corner 3:

Row 1 (RS): using **yarn A**, sl st in 2-ch sp closest to the left of any 2 sl st made in round 8, ch 2, [1 dc in next st, (1 sl st, ch 2, 1 dc) in next st] five times, 1 dc in next st, sl st in next 2-ch sp (6 blocks).

Fasten off **yarn A**.

Row 2 (RS): using **yarn C**, sl st in first 2-ch sp of row 1, [1 dc in next st, (1 dc, ch 2, 1 sl st) in next st] four times, 1 dc in next st, ch 2, sl st in next 2-ch sp (5 blocks).

Fasten off **yarn C**.

Row 3 (RS): using **yarn D**, sl st in first 2-ch sp of row 2, [1 dc in next st, (1 dc, ch 2, 1 sl st) in next st] three times, 1 dc in next st, ch 2, sl st in next 2-ch sp (4 blocks).

Fasten off **yarn D**.

Row 4 (RS): using **yarn B,** sl st in first 2-ch sp of row 3, [1 dc in next st, (1 dc, ch 2, 1 sl st) in next st] twice, 1 dc in next st, ch 2, sl st in next 2-ch sp (3 blocks).

Fasten off **yarn B**.

Row 5 (RS): using **yarn E,** sl st in first 2-ch sp of row 4, 1 dc in next st, [1 dc, ch 2, 1 sl st] in next st, 1 dc in next st, ch 2, sl st in next 2-ch sp (2 blocks).

Fasten off **yarn E**.

Row 6 (RS): using **yarn F**, sl st in first 2-ch sp of row 5, 1 dc in next st, ch 2, sl st in next 2-ch sp (1 block).

Fasten off **yarn F**.

Corner 4: rep instructions as per corner 3, starting in 2-ch sp closest to the left of the second pair of 2 sl st made in round 8.

BORDER

Round 1 (RS): using **yarn B**, in last 2-ch sp made in any corner, ch 1 (does not count as st throughout), 1 sc in same sp, [2 sc in each of next six 2-ch sp, 1 sc in each of next 2 sl st, 2 sc in each of next six 2-ch sp, 1 sc in last 2-ch sp, ch 2, 2 hdc in next dc, 1 hdc in each of next 24 dc, 2 hdc in last dc, ch 2, 1 sc in next 2-ch sp] twice, omit final [1 sc in next 2-ch sp] on last rep, sl st in beginning sc (112 sts).

Round 2 (RS): ch 1, 1 sc in same st, 1 sc in each of next 27 sts, 3 sc in next 2-ch sp, [1 sc in each of next 28 sts, 3 sc in next 2-ch sp] three times, sl st in beginning sc (124 sts).

Fasten off **yarn B**.

Weave in ends and block.

NOTES: Due to the nature of the stitches in this square, it is essential to block your final piece for the best results.

This square consists of five different components: the main body is worked in rounds to create a diamond shape, then each of the four corners is worked in rows to complete the square.

Skip all 2-ch sp unless otherwise instructed.

Rainbow Relief

An interesting square with a raised, 3D effect that is fun to crochet.

Using yarn A, start with a magic ring.

Round 1 (RS): ch 3 (counts as 1 dc throughout), 11 dc into ring, sl st in third ch of beginning ch 3 (12 sts).

Fasten off yarn A.

Round 2 (RS): using yarn B, 1 sbpsc around any st, ch 1, [1 bpsc around next st, ch 1] eleven times, sl st in sbpsc (12 bpsc, 12 x ch sp).

Fasten off yarn B.

Round 3 (RS): using yarn C, in any ch sp, ch 3, 2 dc in same ch sp, skip bpsc, [3 dc in next ch sp, skip bpsc] eleven times, sl st in third ch of beginning ch 3 (36 sts).

Fasten off yarn C.

Round 4 (RS): using yarn B, 1 sbpsc around any st, 1 bpsc around each st, sl st in sbpsc (36 sts).

Fasten off yarn B.

Round 5 (RS): using yarn D, in any st, ch 2 (counts as 1 hdc), 1 hdc in same st, [1 hdc in each of next 2 sts, 2 hdc in next st] twelve times, omit 2 hdc on last rep, sl st in second ch of beginning ch 2 (48 sts).

Fasten off yarn D.

Round 6 (RS): rep round 4 (48 sts).

Round 7 (RS): using yarn E, in any st, ch 4 (counts as 1 tr), [1 tr, ch 2, 2 tr] in same st, [1 dc in each of next 2 sts, 1 hdc in next st, 1 sc in each of next 5 sts, 1 hdc in next st, 1 dc in each of next 2 sts, (2 tr, ch 2, 2 tr) in next st] four times, omit [2 tr, ch 2, 2 tr] on last rep, sl st in fourth ch of beginning ch 4 (60 sts).

Fasten off yarn E.

Round 8 (RS): using yarn B, in any 2-ch sp, ch 1 (does not count as st), [(1 sc, ch 2, 1 sc) in 2-ch sp, 1 bpsc in each st until next 2-ch sp] four times, sl st in beginning sc (68 sts).

Fasten off yarn B.

Round 9 (RS): using yarn F, in any 2-ch sp, ch 2 (does not count as st), [(2 hdc, ch 2, 2 hdc) in 2-ch sp, 1 hdc in each of next 17 sts] four times, sl st in beginning hdc (84 sts).

Fasten off yarn F.

Round 10 (RS): rep round 8 (92 sts).

Round 11 (RS): using yarn G, in any 2-ch sp, ch 2 (does not count as st), [(1 hdc, ch 2, 1 hdc) in 2-ch sp, 1 hdc in each of next 23 sts] four times, sl st in beginning hdc (100 sts).

Fasten off yarn G.

Round 12 (RS): rep round 8 (108 sts).

Round 13 (RS): using yarn H, in any 2-ch sp, ch 2 (does not count as st), [(1 hdc, ch 1, 1 hdc) in 2-ch sp, 1 hdc in each of next 27 sts] four times, sl st in beginning hdc (116 sts).

Fasten off yarn H.

Weave in ends and block.

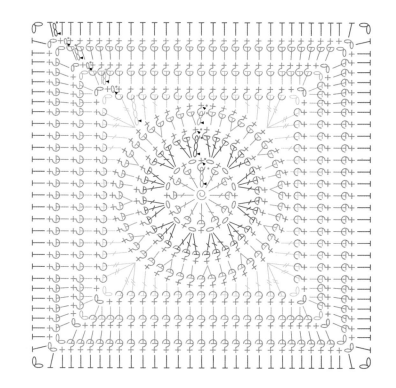

HOOK SIZE	BLOCK SIZE
US G/6 (4mm)	6 x 6in (15 x 15cm)

TECHNIQUES

Beginning a row/round with a standing stitch
(see notes at end of pattern)

YARN/COLORS

Sample uses Scheepjes Softfun

A = Rose (#2514)	E = Canary (#2518)
B = Snow (#2412)	F = Apple (#2516)
C = Candy Apple (#2410)	G = Bright Turquoise (#2423)
D = Tangerine (#2427)	H = Heath (#2493)

STITCHES

ch—chain	bpsc—back post single crochet
sl st—slip stitch	
sc—single crochet	sbpsc—standing back post single crochet
hdc—half double crochet	
dc—double crochet	
tr—treble crochet	

MIX AND MATCH

 +

Page 14 + Page 30

CHART KEY

For symbol key, see page 122

NOTES: Save yourself a bunch of ends by keeping **yarn B** attached the whole time. Once you've finished a round using this color, close the round as normal. Instead of cutting the yarn, keep it attached and hanging from the WS of the square. When it's time to use it again, pick it up with your hook and join it back in the corner space.

To work standing back post single crochet, attach yarn to hook, working around the stem of desired stitch, insert hook from back to front, around the post and to the back again, yarn over and pull yarn through both loops.

HOOK SIZE	BLOCK SIZE
US G/6 (4mm)	6 x 6in (15 x 15cm)

TECHNIQUES

Beginning a row/round with a standing stitch
(see note at end of pattern)

Working over/into previous rounds/rows
(see page 119)

YARN/COLORS

Sample uses Scheepjes Softfun

A = Bumblebee (#2634)

B = Cool Blue (#2603)

C = Snow (#2412)

D = Violet (#2519)

E = Hot Pink (#2495)

F = Cantaloupe (#2652)

STITCHES

ch—chain

sl st—slip stitch

sc—single crochet

hdc—half double crochet

dc—double crochet

fpdc—front post double crochet

sfpdc—standing front post double crochet

MIX AND MATCH

Page 38 ✛ Page 94

CHART KEY

For symbol key, see page 122

Using **yarn A**, start with a magic ring.

Round 1 (RS): ch 3 (counts as 1 dc throughout), 15 dc into ring, sl st in third ch of beginning ch 3 (16 sts).

Round 2 (RS): ch 3, 1 dc in same st, 2 dc in each st around, sl st in third ch of beginning ch 3 (32 sts).

Round 3 (RS): ch 6 (counts as 1 dc, ch 3), skip next st, [1 dc in next st, ch 3, skip next st] fifteen times, sl st in third ch of beginning ch 6 (16 dc, 16 x 3-ch sp).

Fasten off **yarn A**.

Round 4 (RS): using **yarn B**, in any 3-ch sp, ch 3, 2 dc in same sp, [skip next st, 4 dc in next 3-ch sp, skip next st, 3 dc in next 3-ch sp] eight times, omit 3 dc on last rep, skip last st, sl st in third ch of beginning ch 3 (56 sts).

Fasten off **yarn B**.

NOTE: For the next round, stitches are made around round 3 dc stitches.

Round 5 (RS): using **yarn A**, 1 sfpdc around any dc, ch 8, skip next 3-ch sp and dc, [skip next 3-ch sp, 1 fpdc around next dc, ch 8, skip next 3-ch sp and dc] seven times,

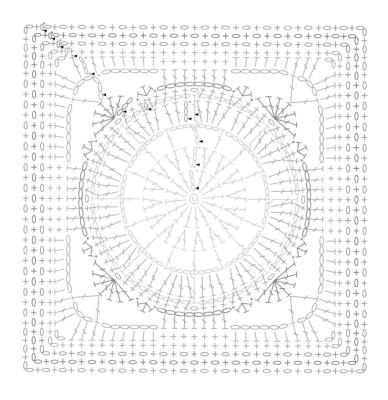

Round 9 (RS): sl st in next 3-ch sp, ch 3, [1 dc, ch 2, 2 dc] in same 3-ch sp, [1 dc in next st, 6 hdc in 6-ch sp, 1 sc in each of next 7 sts, 6 hdc in 6-ch sp, 1 dc in next st, (2 dc, ch 2, 2 dc) in 3-ch sp] four times, omit [2 dc, ch 2, 2 dc] on last rep, sl st in third ch of beginning ch 3 (100 sts).

Round 10 (RS): sl st in next st, sl st in next 2-ch sp, ch 1, [[1 sc, ch 2, 1 sc] in 2-ch sp, 1 sc in each of next 25 sts] four times, sl st in beginning sc (108 sts).

Fasten off **yarn B**.

Round 11 (RS): using **yarn D**, in any 2-ch sp, ch 1, [[1 sc, ch 2, 1 sc] in 2-ch sp, ch 1, skip next st, (1 sc in next st, ch 1, skip next st) thirteen times] four times, sl st in beginning sc (60 sc, 56 x ch sp, 4 x 2-ch sp).

Fasten off **yarn D**.

Round 12 (RS): using **yarn E**, in any 2-ch sp, ch 1, [[1 sc, ch 2, 1 sc] in 2-ch sp, ch 1, skip next st, (1 sc in next st, ch 1, skip next st) fourteen times] four times, sl st in beginning sc (64 sc, 60 x ch sp, 4 x 2-ch sp).

Fasten off **yarn E**.

Round 13 (RS): using **yarn F**, in any 2-ch sp, ch 1, [[1 sc, ch 2, 1 sc] in 2-ch sp, ch 1, skip next st, (1 sc in next st, ch 1, skip next st) fifteen times] four times, sl st in beginning sc (68 sc, 64 x ch sp, 4 x 2-ch sp).

Fasten off **yarn F**.

Weave in ends and block.

NOTE: To work standing front post double crochet, attach yarn to hook, wrap yarn around hook once, working around the stem of desired stitch, insert hook from front to back, around the post and to the front again, yarn over and pull yarn through two loops, yarn over and pull through remaining loops.

sl st in sfpdc (8 fpdc, 8 x 8-ch sp).

Fasten off **yarn A**.

NOTE: For the next round, stitches are worked into round 4. Work over round 5 8-ch and skip all fpdc.

Round 6 (RS): using **yarn B**, in second dc of any 4 dc round 4 group, ch 1 (does not count as st throughout), 1 sc in same st, 1 sc in each of next 2 sts, [ch 1, 1 sc in each of next 3 sts, 2 sc in next st, 1 sc in each of next 3 sts] eight times, omit 3 sc on last rep, sl st in beginning sc (64 sc, 8 x ch sp). Fasten off **yarn B**.

Round 7 (RS): using **yarn C**, in any ch sp, ch 3, 6 dc in same sp, [skip next 2 sts, sl st in next st, 3 hdc in next st, sl st in next st, ch 8, skip next 3 sts, skip ch sp, skip next 3 sts, sl st in next st, 3 hdc in next st, sl st in next st, skip next 2 sts,

7 dc in next st] four times, omit 7 dc on last rep, sl st in third ch of beginning ch 3 (4 clouds, 4 x 8-ch sp).

Fasten off **yarn C**.

NOTE: For the next round, some stitches are worked into round 7 and some are worked over round 7 and into round 6.

Round 8 (RS): using **yarn B**, in fourth dc of any round 7 group, ch 6 (counts as 1 dc, ch 3), 1 dc in same st, [ch 6, **working into round 6**: 1 dc in each of next 3 sts, 1 dc in ch sp, 1 dc in each of next 3 sts (remember to work over round 7 ch), ch 6, **working into round 7**: [(1 dc, ch 3, 1 dc) in fourth dc of 7 dc group] four times, omit [1 dc, ch 3, 1 dc] on last rep, sl st in third ch of beginning ch 6 (36 dc, 8 x 6-ch sp, 4 x 3-ch sp).

HOOK SIZE	BLOCK SIZE
US E/4 (3.5mm)	6 x 6in (15 x 15cm)

TECHNIQUES

Changing color on row/round (see page 121)

Working with multiple colors at the same time/intarsia crochet (see page 121)

YARN/COLORS

Sample uses Scheepjes Softfun

A = Cool Blue (#2603)

B = Snow (#2412)

C = Botanical (#2615)

D = Mint (#2640)

E = Soft Lime (#2638)

F = Canary (#2518)

G = Cantaloupe (#2652)

H = Soft Coral (#2636)

I = Salmon (#2449)

STITCHES

ch—chain

sl st—slip stitch

hdc—half double crochet

dc—double crochet

MIX AND MATCH

Page 14 + Page 72 + Page 30

CHART KEY

For symbol key, see page 122

Jell-O and Ice Cream

This fun design is reminiscent of the kids' party favorite.

Using **yarn A**, ch 4 and join with sl st in first ch made to form a ring.

Round 1 (WS): ch 3 (counts as 1 dc throughout), [2 dc, ch 2, 3 dc] into ring, ch 1; using **yarn B**, ch 1, [3 dc, ch 2, 3 dc] into ring, 1 hdc in third ch of beginning ch 3 (hdc counts as ch 2 throughout), turn (12 sts, 4 x 2-ch sp).

Fasten off **yarn A**.

Round 2 (RS): ch 3, 1 dc in same place, 1 dc in each of next 3 sts, [2 dc, ch 3, 2 dc] in 2-ch sp, 1 dc in each of next 3 sts, 2 dc in 2-ch sp, ch 1; using **yarn C**, ch 1, 2 dc in same ch sp, 1 dc in each of next 3 sts, [2 dc, ch 2, 2 dc] in next ch sp, 1 dc in each of next 3 sts, 2 dc in ch sp; using **yarn D**, 1 hdc in third ch of beginning ch 3, turn.

Fasten off **yarn C**.

Round 3 (WS): ch 3, 1 dc in same place, 1 dc in each of next 7 sts, [2 dc, ch 2, 2 dc] in

ch sp, 1 dc in each of next 7 sts, 2 dc in ch sp, ch 1; using **yarn B**, ch 1, 2 dc in same ch sp, 1 dc in each of next 7 sts, [2 dc, ch 2, 2 dc] in ch sp, 1 dc in each of next 7 sts, 2 dc in ch sp, 1 hdc in third ch of beginning ch 3, turn. Fasten off **yarn D**.

Round 4 (RS): ch 3, 1 dc in same place, 1 dc in each of next 11 sts, [2 dc, ch 2, 2 dc] in ch sp, 1 dc in each of next 11 sts, 2 dc in ch sp, ch 1; using **yarn E**, ch 1, 2 dc in same ch sp, 1 dc in each of next 11 sts, [2 dc, ch 2, 2 dc] in ch sp, 1 dc in each of next 11 sts, 2 dc in ch sp; using **yarn F,** 1 hdc in third ch of beginning ch 3, turn. Fasten off **yarn E**.

Round 5 (WS): ch 3, 1 dc in same ch sp, 1 dc in each of next 15 sts, [2 dc, ch 2, 2 dc] in ch sp, 1 dc in each of next 15 sts, 2 dc in ch sp, ch 1; using **yarn B**, ch 1, 2 dc in same ch sp, 1 dc in each of next 15 sts, [2 dc, ch 2, 2 dc] in ch sp, 1 dc in each of next 15 sts, 2 dc in ch sp, 1 hdc in third ch of beginning ch 3, turn. Fasten off **yarn F**.

Round 6 (RS): ch 3, 1 dc in same ch sp, 1 dc in each of next 19 sts, [2 dc, ch 2, 2 dc] in ch sp, 1 dc in each of next 19 sts, 2 dc in ch sp, ch 1; using **yarn G**, ch 1, 2 dc in same ch sp, 1 dc in each of next 19 sts, [2 dc, ch 2, 2 dc] in ch sp, 1 dc in each of next 19 sts, 2 dc in ch sp; using **yarn H**, 1 hdc in third ch of beginning ch 3, turn. Fasten off **yarn G**.

Round 7 (WS): ch 3, 1 dc in same ch sp, 1 dc in each of next 23 sts, [2 dc, ch 2, 2 dc] in ch

sp, 1 dc in each of next 23 sts, 2 dc in ch sp, ch 1; using **yarn B**, ch 1, 2 dc in same ch sp, 1 dc in each of next 23 sts, [2 dc, ch 2, 2 dc] in ch sp, 1 dc in each of next 23 sts, 2 dc in ch sp, 1 hdc in third ch of beginning ch 3, turn. Fasten off **yarn H**.

Round 8 (RS): ch 3, 1 dc in same ch sp, 1 dc in each of next 27 sts, [2 dc, ch 2, 2 dc] in ch sp, 1 dc in each of next 27 sts, 2 dc in ch sp, ch 1; using **yarn I**, ch 1, 2 dc in same ch sp, 1 dc in each of next 27 sts, [2 dc, ch 2, 2 dc] in ch sp, 1 dc in each of next 27 sts, 2 dc in ch sp, ch 2,

sl st in third ch of beginning ch 3. Fasten off **yarn B** and **yarn I**.

Weave in ends and block.

NOTES: When joining at the end of a round, you'll be joining by working 1 hdc in the top ch of the beginning ch. This hdc counts as ch 2 throughout.
When not in use, leave **yarn B** at the back of your work.

Multicolored Target

When you finish this gorgeous square, you'll feel as though you have hit the bull's-eye.

Using **yarn A**, ch 4 and join with sl st in first ch made to form a ring.

Round 1 (RS): ch 3 (counts as 1 dc throughout), 11 dc into ring, sl st in third ch of beginning ch 3 (12 sts).
Fasten off **yarn A**.

Round 2 (RS): using **yarn B**, ch 3, 1 dc in same place, 2 dc in each of next 11 sts, sl st in third ch of beginning ch 3 (24 sts).
Fasten off **yarn B**.

Round 3 (RS): using **yarn C**, ch 3, 1 dc in same place, [1 dc in next st, 2 dc in next st] eleven times, 1 dc in last st, sl st in third ch of beginning ch 3 (36 sts).
Fasten off **yarn C**.

Round 4 (RS): using **yarn D**, ch 3, 1 dc in next st, [2 dc in next st, 1 dc in each of next 2 sts] eleven times, 2 dc in last st, sl st in third ch of beginning ch 3 (48 sts).
Fasten off **yarn D**.

Round 5 (RS): using **yarn E**, ch 3, 1 dc in same place, [1 dc in each of next 3 sts, 2 dc in next st] eleven times, 1 dc in each of next 3 sts, sl st in third ch of beginning ch 3 (60 sts).
Fasten off **yarn E**.

Round 6 (RS): using **yarn F**, ch 1 (does not count as st throughout), 1 sc in same place, [1 sc in each of next 4 sts, 1 hdc in each of next 2 sts, 1 dc in each of next 2 sts, (1 dc, 1 tr) in next st, ch 2, (1 tr, 1 dc) in next st, 1 dc in each of next 2 sts, 1 hdc in each of next 2 sts, 1 sc in next st] four times, omit 1 sc on last rep, sl st in beginning sc (68 sts, 4 x ch sp).

Round 7 (RS): ch 3, [1 dc in each st to corner ch sp, (1 dc, 1 tr, ch 1, 1 tr, 1 dc) in ch sp] four times, 1 dc in each of next 6 sts, sl st in third ch of beginning ch 3 (84 sts, 4 x ch sp).
Fasten off **yarn F**.

Round 8 (RS): using **yarn A**, in corner ch sp, ch 1, [(1 sc, ch 2, 1 sc) in ch sp, 1 sc in each st to next corner ch sp] four times, sl st in beginning sc (92 sts, 4 x ch sp).
Fasten off **yarn A**.

Round 9 (RS): rep round 8 using **yarn B** (100 sts, 4 x ch sp).

Round 10 (RS): rep round 8 using **yarn C** (108 sts, 4 x ch sp).

Round 11 (RS): rep round 8 using **yarn D** (116 sts, 4 x ch sp).

Round 12 (RS): using **yarn E**, in corner ch sp, ch 1, [(1 sc, 1 hdc, 1 sc) in ch sp, 1 sc in each st to next corner ch sp] four times, sl st in beginning sc (128 sts).
Fasten off **yarn E**.

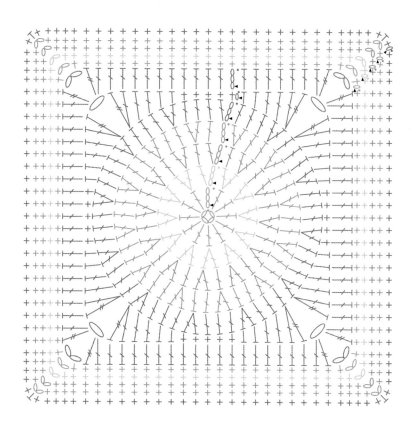

Weave in ends and block.

NOTE: To keep the corners neat, from round 8 onward, begin each round in the corner directly opposite to the one in the previous round.

HOOK SIZE	BLOCK SIZE
US E/4 (3.5mm)	6 x 6in (15 x 15cm)

YARN/COLORS
Sample uses Paintbox Cotton DK
A = Lime Green (#429)
B = Buttercup Yellow (#423)
C = Blood Orange (#420)
D = Bubblegum Pink (#451)
E = Lipstick Pink (#452)
F = Misty Grey (#404)

STITCHES
ch—chain
sl st—slip stitch
sc—single crochet
hdc—half double crochet
dc—double crochet
tr—treble crochet

MIX AND MATCH

Page 40 + Page 68

CHART KEY
For symbol key, see page 122

HOOK SIZE	BLOCK SIZE
US G/6 (4mm)	6 x 6in (15 x 15cm)

TECHNIQUES

Working over/into previous rounds/rows
(see page 119)

YARN/COLORS

Sample uses Scheepjes Softfun

A = Soft Lime (#2638)

B = Light Rose (#2513)

C = Coral (#2607)

D = Apple (#2516)

E = Snow (#2412)

STITCHES

ch—chain	dc-2-cl—cluster made
sl st—slip stitch	of double crochet
sc—single crochet	2 sts together
hdc—half double	tr-3-cl—cluster made
crochet	of treble crochet
dc—double crochet	3 sts together
tr—treble crochet	tr-2-cl—cluster made
fpdc—front post	of treble crochet
double crochet	2 sts together

MIX AND MATCH

Page 30 + Page 36

CHART KEY

For symbol key, see page 122

Acid Brights Flower

This square would make a striking central point of any design.

Using **yarn A**, ch 4 and join with sl st in first ch made to form a ring.

Round 1 (RS): ch 3 (counts as 1 dc throughout), 15 dc into ring, sl st in third ch of beginning ch 3 (16 sts).

Fasten off **yarn A**.

Round 2 (RS): using **yarn B**, ch 1 (does not count as st throughout), 1 sc in same place, [ch 2, skip 1 st, 1 sc in next st] seven times, ch 2, sl st in beginning sc (8 sts, 8 x 2-ch sp).

Round 3 (RS): sl st in ch sp, [(1 sc, ch 2, dc-2-cl, ch 2, 1 sc) in ch sp, skip 1 sc] eight times, sl st in beginning sc (8 petals).

Fasten off **yarn B**.

Round 4 (RS): using **yarn C**, in any dc-2-cl, ch 1, [1 sc in dc-2-cl, ch 2, 1 fpdc around sc on round 2, ch 2] eight times, sl st in beginning sc (8 sc, 8 fpdc, 16 x 2-ch sp).

Fasten off **yarn C**.

Round 5 (RS): using **yarn A**, in any fpdc, ch 1, [1 sc in fpdc, ch 3] eight times, sl st in beginning sc (8 sts, 8 x 3-ch sp).

Round 6 (RS): sl st in ch sp, ch 1, [(1 sc, ch 3, tr-3-cl, ch 3, 1 sc) in ch sp, skip next sc] eight times, sl st in beginning sc (8 petals).

Fasten off **yarn A**.

Round 7 (RS): using **yarn C**, in any tr-3-cl, ch 1, [1 sc in tr-3-cl, ch 3, 1 fpdc around sc on round 5, ch 3] eight times, sl st in beginning sc (8 sc, 8 fpdc, 16 x ch sp).

Fasten off **yarn C**.

Round 8 (RS): using **yarn D**, in any fpdc, [ch 3, 1 tr, ch 4, tr-2-cl] in same place, [ch 2, (tr-2-cl, ch 4, tr-2-cl) in next fpdc] seven times, ch 2, sl st in beginning tr-2-cl (16 tr-2-cl, 8 x 4-ch sp, 8 x 2-ch sp).

Fasten off **yarn D**.

Round 9 (RS): using **yarn E**, in any 4-ch sp, ch 1, [5 sc in 4-ch sp, (1 hdc, 1 hdc in sc on round 7 working over 2-ch sp, 1 hdc) in 2-ch sp] eight times, sl st in beginning sc.

Round 10 (RS): 1 sl st in each of next 2 sts to third of 5 sc, ch 4 (counts as 1 tr throughout), 1 dc in same place, [1 dc in each of next 3 sts, 1 hdc in each of next 3 sts, 1 sc in each of next 3 sts, 1 hdc in each of next 3 sts, 1 dc in each of next 3 sts, (1 dc, 1 tr, ch 2, 1 tr, 1 dc) in next st] four times, omit [1 tr, 1 dc] on last rep, 1 hdc in fourth ch of beginning ch 4 (hdc counts as ch 2 throughout).

Round 11 (RS): ch 3, 1 dc in same place, [1 dc in each st to next 2-ch sp, (2 dc, ch 2, 2 dc) in ch sp] four times, omit [ch 2, 2 dc] on last rep, 1 hdc in third ch of beginning ch 3.

Round 12 (RS): rep round 11.

Fasten off **yarn E**.

Weave in ends and block.

Ombré Cross

The popcorn stitches create a cross that stands out from the double crochet background.

Using **yarn A**, ch 8 and join with sl st in first ch made to form a ring.

Round 1 (RS): 1 beg pc into ring, [ch 5, 1 pc5 into ring] three times, ch 5, sl st in beg pc (4 pc5).

Fasten off **yarn A**.

Round 2 (RS): using **yarn B**, in 5-ch sp, ch 3, 1 dc in same place, [1 dc in pc, (2 dc; using **yarn C**, ch 2, 1 pc5; using **yarn B**, ch 2, 2 dc) in next 5-ch sp] four times, omit [ch 2, 2 dc] on last rep, 1 hdc in third ch of beginning ch 3 (hdc counts as ch 2 throughout) (20 dc, 4 pc5, 8 x 2-ch sp).

Fasten off **yarn C**.

Round 3 (RS): using **yarn B**, ch 3, 1 dc in same place, [1 dc in each of next 5 sts, (2 dc; using **yarn D**, ch 2, 1 pc5; using **yarn B**, ch 2, 2 dc) in next 5-ch sp] four times, omit [ch 2, 2 dc] on last rep, 1 hdc in third ch of beginning ch 3 (36 dc, 4 pc5, 8 x 2-ch sp).

Fasten off **yarn D**.

Round 4 (RS): using **yarn B**, ch 3, 1 dc in same place, [1 dc in each of next 9 sts, (2 dc; using **yarn E**, ch 2, 1 pc5; using **yarn B**, ch 2, 2 dc) in next 5-ch sp] four times, omit [ch 2, 2 dc] on last rep, 1 hdc in third ch of beginning ch 3 (52 dc, 4 pc5, 8 x 2-ch sp).

Fasten off **yarn E**.

Round 5 (RS): using **yarn B**, ch 3, 1 dc in same place, [1 dc in each of next 13 sts, (2 dc; using **yarn F**, ch 2, 1 pc5; using **yarn B**, ch 2, 2 dc) in next 5-ch sp] four times, omit

[ch 2, 2 dc] on last rep, 1 hdc in third ch of beginning ch 3 (68 dc, 4 pc5, 8 x 2-ch sp).

Fasten off **yarn F**.

Round 6 (RS): using **yarn B**, ch 3, 1 dc in same place, [1 dc in each of next 17 sts, (2 dc; using **yarn G**, ch 2, 1 pc5; using **yarn B**, ch 2, 2 dc) in next 5-ch sp] four times, omit [ch 2, 2 dc] on last rep, 1 hdc in third ch of beginning ch 3 (84 dc, 4 pc5, 8 x 2-ch sp).

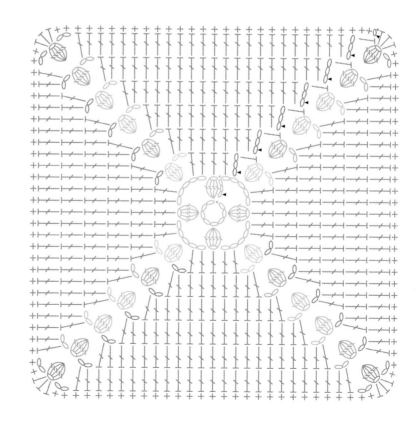

Fasten off **yarn G**.

Round 7 (RS): using **yarn B**, ch 3, 1 dc in same place, [1 dc in each of next 21 sts, (2 dc; using **yarn H**, ch 2, 1 pc5; using **yarn B**, ch 2, 2 dc) in next 5-ch sp] four times, omit [ch 2, 2 dc] on last rep, 1 hdc in third ch of beginning ch 3, (100 dc, 4 pc5, 8 x 2-ch sp).

Fasten off **yarn H**.

Round 8 (RS): using **yarn B**, ch 1 (does not

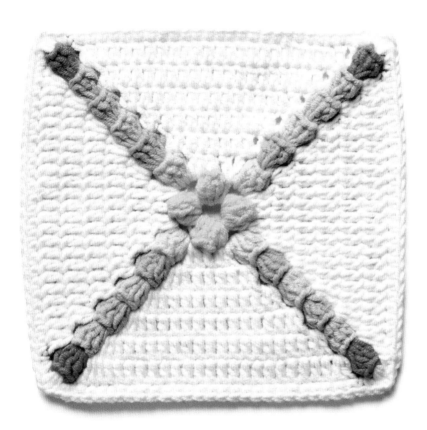

count as st), [2 sc in ch sp, 1 sc in each st to next ch sp, 2 sc in ch sp, 3 hdc in pc5] four times, sl st in beginning sc (128 sts). Fasten off **yarn B**.

Weave in ends and block.

HOOK SIZE	BLOCK SIZE
US E/4 (3.5mm)	6 x 6in (15 x 15cm)

TECHNIQUES

Changing color on row/round (see page 121)

Working with multiple colors at the same time/ tapestry crochet (see page 121)

YARN/COLORS

Sample uses Scheepjes Softfun

A = Canary (#2518)   F = Sky (#2613)

B = Snow (#2412)   G = Cool Blue (#2603)

C = Soft Lime (#2638)   H = Bright Turquoise

D = Apple (#2516)   (#2423)

E = Mint (#2640)

STITCHES

ch—chain

sl st—slip stitch

sc—single crochet

hdc—half double crochet

dc—double crochet

pc5—5 dc popcorn stitch (ch 1 to secure)

beg pc5—beginning 5 dc popcorn stitch: ch 3 (counts as 1 dc), 4 dc, close as regular pc

MIX AND MATCH

Page 42   +   Page 82

CHART KEY

For symbol key, see page 122

Warm Tones

This floral design brings a modern twist to the granny square.

———

Using **yarn A**, ch 4 and join with sl st in first ch made to form a ring.

Round 1 (RS): ch 1, 6 sc into ring, sl st in first sc (6 sts).

Round 2 (RS): ch 1, 2 sc in each st around, sl st in first sc (12 sts).

Fasten off **yarn A**.

Round 3 (RS): using **yarn B**, ch 2, 1 dc in next st (counts as dc-2-cl), ch 2, [dc-2-cl over next 2 sts, ch 2] eleven times, sl st in beginning dc-2-cl (12 sts, 12 x 2-ch sp).

Fasten off **yarn B**.

Round 4 (RS): using **yarn C**, in ch sp, beg dc-3-cl, ch 3, [dc-3-cl in next ch sp, ch 3] eleven times, sl st in beginning dc-3-cl (12 dc-3-cl, 12 x 3-ch sp).

Fasten off **yarn C**.

Round 5 (RS): using **yarn D**, in ch sp, beg cg

in same sp, [ch 2, skip next ch sp, 1 sc in next dc-3-cl, ch 2, skip next ch sp and st, cg in next ch sp] four times, omit 1 cg on last rep, sl st in first dc of beg cg (4 cg, 4 sc, 8 x 2-ch sp). Fasten off yarn D.

Round 6 (RS): using yarn E, in corner 3-ch sp, beg cg in same place; [using yarn F, 2 dc in next ch sp, 3 dc in next ch sp, 1 fpdc around next dc-3-cl on round 4, 3 dc in next ch sp, 2 dc in next ch sp; using yarn E, cg in next ch sp] four times, omit 1 cg and final color change on last rep, sl st in first dc of beg cg (4 cg in yarn E, 40 dc, 4 fpdc). Fasten off yarn E.

Round 7 (RS): using yarn D, in corner 3-ch sp, beg cg in same place; [using yarn F, 2 dc in next ch sp, 1 dc in each st to next ch sp, 2 dc in ch sp; using yarn D, cg in ch sp] four times, omit 1 cg and final color change on last rep, sl st in first dc of beg cg (4 cg in yarn D, 60 dc in yarn F). Fasten off yarn D.

Round 8 (RS): rep round 7 using yarn B instead of yarn D (4 cg in yarn B, 76 dc in yarn F).

Round 9: rep round 7 using yarn A instead of yarn D (4 cg in yarn A, 92 dc in yarn F).

Weave in ends and block.

Technicolor Square

The gorgeous colors in this square create a rainbow of design possibilities.

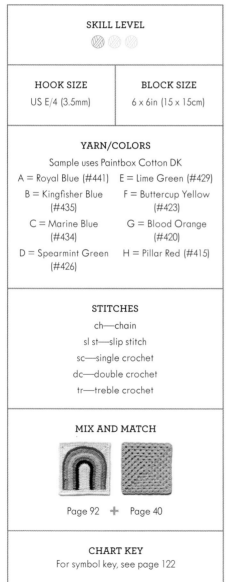

SKILL LEVEL
◍ ◍ ◍

HOOK SIZE	BLOCK SIZE
US E/4 (3.5mm)	6 x 6in (15 x 15cm)

YARN/COLORS

Sample uses Paintbox Cotton DK

A = Royal Blue (#441)   E = Lime Green (#429)

B = Kingfisher Blue (#435)   F = Buttercup Yellow (#423)

C = Marine Blue (#434)   G = Blood Orange (#420)

D = Spearmint Green (#426)   H = Pillar Red (#415)

STITCHES

ch—chain

sl st—slip stitch

sc—single crochet

dc—double crochet

tr—treble crochet

MIX AND MATCH

Page 92   ✛   Page 40

CHART KEY

For symbol key, see page 122

Using **yarn A**, ch 4 and join with sl st in first ch made to form a ring.

Round 1 (RS): ch 1 (does not count as st throughout), [3 sc into ring, ch 10] four times, sl st in first sc (12 sts, 4 x 10-ch sp).

Fasten off **yarn A**.

Round 2 (RS): using **yarn B**, in next sc, ch 4 (counts as 1 tr throughout), 1 dc in same place, [1 dc in next st, (1 dc, 1 tr) in next st, ch 12, (1 tr, 1 dc) in next st] four times, omit [1 tr, 1 dc] on last rep, sl st in fourth ch of beginning ch 4 (20 sts, 4 x 12-ch sp).

Fasten off **yarn B**.

Round 3 (RS): using **yarn C**, ch 4, 2 dc in same place, [1 dc in each of next 3 sts, (2 dc, 1 tr) in next st, ch 12, (1 tr, 2 dc) in next st] four times, omit [1 tr, 2 dc] on last rep, sl st in fourth ch of beginning ch 4 (36 sts, 4 x 12-ch sp).

Fasten off **yarn C**.

Round 4 (RS): using **yarn D**, ch 4, 2 dc in same place, [1 dc in each of next 7 sts, (2 dc, 1 tr) in next st, ch 12, (1 tr, 2 dc) in next st]

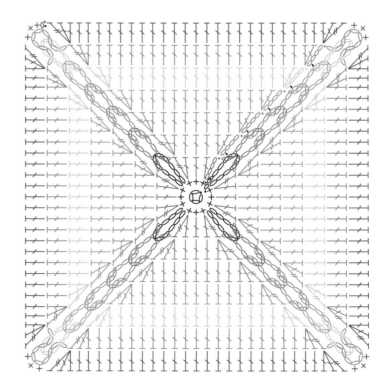

four times, omit [1 tr, 2 dc] on last rep, sl st in fourth ch of beginning ch 4 (52 sts, 4 x 12-ch sp).

Fasten off **yarn D.**

Round 5 (RS): using **yarn E**, ch 4, 2 dc in same place, [1 dc in each of next 11 sts, (2 dc, 1 tr) in next st, ch 12, (1 tr, 2 dc) in next st] four times, omit [1 tr, 2 dc] on last rep, sl st in fourth ch of beginning ch 4 (68 sts, 4 x 12-ch sp).

Fasten off **yarn E.**

Round 6 (RS): using **yarn F**, ch 4, 2 dc in same place, [1 dc in each of next 15 sts, (2 dc, 1 tr) in next st, ch 12, (1 tr, 2 dc) in next st] four

times, omit [1 tr, 2 dc] on last rep, sl st in fourth ch of beginning ch 4 (84 sts, 4 x 12-ch sp).

Fasten off **yarn F.**

Round 7 (RS): using **yarn G**, ch 4, 2 dc in same place, [1 dc in each of next 19 sts, (2 dc, 1 tr) in next st, ch 10, (1 tr, 2 dc) in next st] four times, omit last [1 tr, 2 dc] on last rep, sl st in fourth ch of beginning ch 4 (100 sts, 4 x 10-ch sp).

Fasten off **yarn G.**

Corner chain links: form the corner chain links by pulling the ch 12 from round 2 through the ch 10 of round 1 from the back of your work to the front, rep by pulling

ch 12 from round 3 through ch 12 of round 2, pull ch 12 from round 4 through ch 12 of round 3, pull ch 12 from round 5 through ch 12 of round 4, pull ch 12 from round 6 through ch 12 of round 5, pull ch 10 from round 7 through ch 12 of round 6.

Round 8: using **yarn H**, in corner 10-ch sp of round 7, ch 1, [3 sc in corner ch sp, (1 tr, 2 dc) in next st, 1 dc in each of next 23 sts, (2 dc, 1 tr) in next st] four times, sl st in beginning sc (128 sts).

Fasten off **yarn H.**

Weave in ends and block.

Brighton Rock

These cool marine colors with a pop of sunshine bring to mind a day at the beach.

———

Using **yarn A**, ch 4 and join with sl st in first ch made to form a ring.

Round 1 (RS): ch 5 (counts as 1 dc, ch 2), [1 dc into ring, ch 2] seven times, sl st in third ch of beginning ch 5 (8 sts, 8 x 2-ch sp).

Fasten off **yarn A**.

Round 2 (RS): using **yarn B**, in ch sp, ch 3 (counts as 1 dc throughout), [1 dc, ch 2, 2 dc] in same place, [ch 1, 2 dc in next ch sp, ch 1, (2 dc, ch 2, 2 dc) in next ch sp] three times, ch 1, 2 dc in next ch sp, ch 1, sl st in third ch of beginning ch 3 (24 sts, 4 x 2-ch sp, 8 x ch sp).

Fasten off **yarn B**.

Round 3 (RS): using **yarn C**, in corner 2-ch sp, ch 3, [1 dc, ch 2, 2 dc] in same sp, [skip 2 sts, (2 dc in ch sp, skip 2 sts) twice, (2 dc, ch 2, 2 dc) in next ch sp] four times, omit [2 dc, ch 2, 2 dc] on last rep, sl st in third ch of beginning ch 3 (32 sts, 4 x 2-ch sp).

Fasten off **yarn C**.

Round 4 (RS): using **yarn D**, in corner 2-ch sp, ch 1 (does not count as st throughout), [3 sc in 2-ch sp, 1 sc in each st to next corner 2-ch sp] four times, sl st in beginning sc (44 sts).

Fasten off **yarn D**.

Round 5 (RS): using **yarn E**, in second of 3 sc, ch 3, [1 dc, ch 2, 2 dc] in same place, [1 dc in each st to second of 3 sc in next corner, (2 dc, ch 2, 2 dc) in next st] four times, omit [2 dc, ch 2, 2 dc] on last rep, sl st in third ch of beginning ch 3 (56 sts, 4 x 2-ch sp).

Fasten off **yarn E**.

Round 6 (RS): rep round 4 using **yarn F** (68 sts).

Round 7 (RS): rep round 5 using **yarn G** (80 sts, 4 x 2-ch sp).

Round 8 (RS): rep round 4 using **yarn H** (92 sts).

Round 9 (RS): rep round 5 using **yarn I** (104 sts, 4 x 2-ch sp).

Round 10 (RS): rep round 4 using **yarn J** (116 sts).

Weave in ends and block.

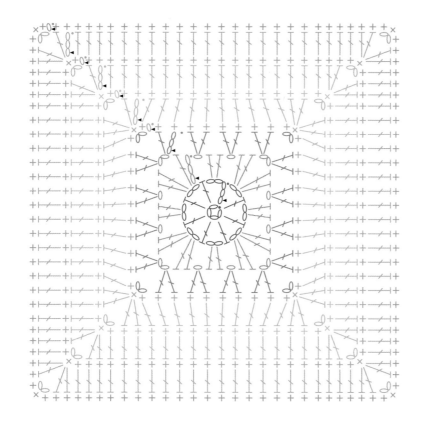

HOOK SIZE	BLOCK SIZE
US G/6 (4mm)	6 x 6in (15 x 15cm)

YARN/COLORS
Sample uses Scheepjes Softfun

A = Azure Blue (#2629)

B = Snow (#2412)

C = Coral (#2607)

D = Soft Coral (#2636)

E = Canary (#2518)

F = Soft Lime (#2638)

G = Mint (#2640)

H = Botanical (#2615)

I = Sky (#2613)

J = Light Blue (#2432)

STITCHES
ch—chain

sl st—slip stitch

sc—single crochet

dc—double crochet

MIX AND MATCH

Page 32 + Page 60

CHART KEY
For symbol key, see page 122

SKILL LEVEL

HOOK SIZE	BLOCK SIZE
US G/6 (4mm)	6 x 6in (15 x 15cm)

TECHNIQUES

Changing color on row/round (see page 121)

Working with multiple colors at the same time/
tapestry crochet (see page 121)

YARN/COLORS

Sample uses Paintbox Cotton DK

A = Buttercup Yellow (#423)

B = Lipstick Pink (#452)

C = Washed Teal (#433)

STITCHES

ch—chain

sl st—slip stitch

sc—single crochet

hdc—half double crochet

dc—double crochet

tr—treble crochet

fptr—front post treble crochet

MIX AND MATCH

Page 30 ✛ Page 50

CHART KEY

For symbol key, see page 122

Four-leaf Flower

The flower is worked first then crocheted into the base square.

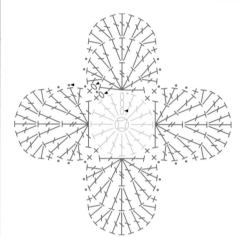

Using **yarn A**, ch 4 and join with sl st in first ch made to form a ring.

Round 1 (RS): ch 3 (counts as 1 dc), 15 dc into ring, sl st in third ch of beginning ch 5 (16 sts).

Fasten off **yarn A**.

Round 2 (RS): using **yarn B**, ch 1 (does not count as st throughout), 1 sc in same place, [skip 1 st, (3 dc, 1 tr, 3 dc) in next st, skip 1 st, 1 sc in next st] four times, omit 1 sc on last rep, sl st in beginning sc (32 sts).

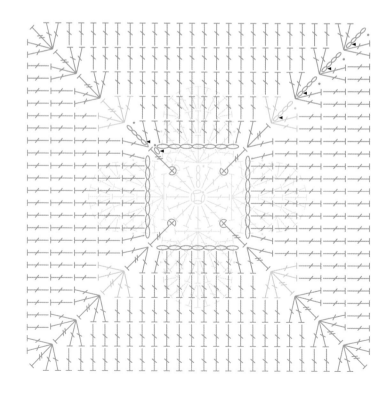

Round 3 (RS): ch 1, 1 sc in same place, [skip 1 st, 3 dc in next st, 2 dc in next st, 3 dc in next st, 2 dc in next st, 3 dc in next st, skip 1 st, 1 sc in next sc] four times, omit 1 sc on last rep, sl st in beginning sc (56 sts).

Round 4 (RS): [1 sl st in each of next 2 sts, 1 sc in next st, 2 hdc in next st, 2 dc in next st, 3 dc in next st, 2 dc in next st, 2 hdc in next st, 1 sc in next st, 1 sl st in each of next 3 sts] four times (52 sts).

Fasten off yarn B.

Round 5 (RS): using yarn C, in third of any 5 sl st, ch 1, [1 fptr around sc of round 2 between two petals, ch 7, ensure ch 7 sits at back of work] four times, sl st in beginning fptr (4 sts, 4 x 7-ch sp).

Round 6 (RS): ch 4 (counts as 1 tr throughout), 1 dc in same place, [8 dc in 7-ch sp, (1 dc, 1 tr, 1 dc) in next st] four times, omit [1 dc, 1 tr, 1 dc] on last rep, sl st in fourth ch of beginning ch 4 (44 sts).

Do not fasten off yarn C.

Round 7 (RS): using yarn A, in corner tr, ch 4, 2 dc in same place; [using yarn C, 1 dc in each of next 10 sts; using yarn A, (2 dc, 1 tr, 2 dc) in next st] four times, omit [1 tr,

2 dc] and final color change on last rep, sl st in fourth ch of beginning ch 4 (60 sts).

Fasten off yarn A.

Round 8 (RS): using yarn C, ch 4, 2 dc in same place, [1 dc in each st to next corner tr, (2 dc, 1 tr, 2 dc) in tr] four times, omit [1 tr, 2 dc] on last rep (72 sts).

Round 9 (RS): rep round 8 (92 sts).

Round 10 (RS): rep round 8 (108 sts).

Fasten off yarn C.

Weave in ends and block.

SKILL LEVEL

HOOK SIZE	BLOCK SIZE
US G/6 (4mm)	6 x 6in (15 x 15cm)

TECHNIQUES

Changing color on row/round (see page 121)

Working with multiple colors at the same time/
intarsia crochet (see page 121)

YARN/COLORS

Sample uses Scheepjes Softfun

A = Peach (#2466)

B = Canary (#2518)

C = Botanical (#2615)

D = Soft Coral (#2636)

E = Mist (#2627)

STITCHES

ch—chain

sl st—slip stitch

sc—single crochet

bo—5 dc bobble stitch

MIX AND MATCH

Page 96 ✚ Page 34

CHART KEY

For symbol key, see page 122

Bobble Beads

This fun square would be perfect as part of a baby blanket.

Using yarn A, ch 28.

Row 1 (WS): ch 1 (does not count as st throughout), 1 sc in second ch from hook, 1 sc in each of next 26 ch, turn (27 sts).

Row 2 (RS): ch 1, 1 dc in each st, turn (27 sts).

Row 3 (WS): ch 1, 1 sc in each of next 13 sts; using yarn B, 1 bo in next st; using yarn A, 1 sc in each of next 13 sts, turn.

Fasten off yarn B.

Rows 4–6: rep row 2.

Row 7 (WS): ch 1, 1 sc in each of next 10 sts; [using yarn C, 1 bo in next st; using yarn A, 1 sc in each of next 2 sts] three times, omit final color change on last rep, 1 sc in each of next 8 sts, turn.

Rows 8–10: rep row 2.

Row 11 (WS): ch 1, 1 sc in each of next 7 sts; [using yarn D, 1 bo in next st; using yarn A,

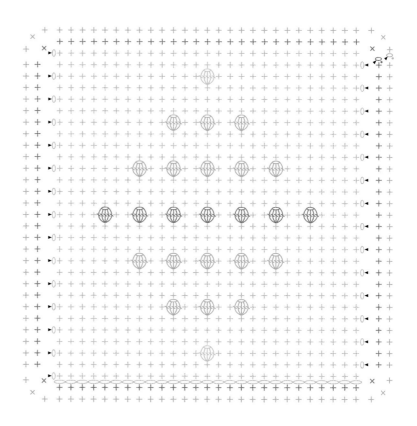

1 sc in each of next 2 sts] five times, omit final color change on last rep, 1 sc in each of next 5 sts, turn.

Rows 12–14: rep row 2.

Row 15 (WS): ch 1, 1 sc in each of next 4 sts; [using **yarn E**, 1 bo in next st; using **yarn A**, 1 sc in each of next 2 sts] seven times, omit final color change on last rep, 1 sc in each of next 2 sts, turn.

Rows 16–18: rep row 2.

Row 19 (WS): rep row 11.

Rows 20–22: rep row 2.

Row 23 (WS): rep row 7.

Rows 24–26: rep row 2.

Row 27 (WS): rep row 3.

Rows 28 and 29: rep row 2.

BORDER

Round 1 (RS): using **yarn E**, in right-hand top corner, ch 1, 3 sc in corner st, 1 sc in each st until next corner, 3 sc in corner, evenly space 25 sc along row ends to next corner, 3 sc in corner, 1 sc in each foundation ch to next corner, 3 sc in corner, evenly space 25 sc along row ends to next corner, sl st in beginning sc (112 sts—25 sts between each corner group of 3 sts).

Fasten off **yarn E**.

Round 2 (RS): using **yarn C**, in second of any 3 sc in corner, ch 1, [3 sc in corner st, 1 sc in each st to next corner] four times, sl st in beginning sc (120 sts).

Fasten off **yarn C**.

Weave in ends and block.

NOTES: Bobble stitches are worked on the wrong side but "pop out" on the right side. To change color when working a bobble, change color on the last yarn over when closing the stitch.

SKILL LEVEL

HOOK SIZE	BLOCK SIZE
US G/6 (4mm)	6 x 6in (15 x 15cm)

TECHNIQUES

Changing color on row/round (see page 121)

Working with multiple colors at the same time/ intarsia crochet (see page 121)

YARN/COLORS

Sample uses Scheepjes Softfun

A = Snow (#2412)

B = Orchid (#2657)

C = Violet (#2519)

D = Cool Blue (#2603)

E = Botanical (#2615)

F = Mint (#2640)

G = Apple (#2516)

H = Soft Lime (#2638)

I = Canary (#2518)

STITCHES

ch—chain   bo—5 dc bobble stitch

sl st—slip stitch

sc—single crochet

MIX AND MATCH

Page 22 + Page 42

CHART KEY

For symbol key, see page 122

Cool-toned Triangle

The use of cool colors in this design creates a striking square.

Using yarn A, ch 28.

Row 1 (RS): ch 1 (does not count as st throughout), 1 sc in second ch from hook, 1 sc each of next 26 ch, turn (27 sts).

Row 2 (WS): ch 1, 1 sc in each of next 24 sts; using yarn B, 1 bo in next st; using yarn A, 1 sc in each of next 2 sts, turn (27 sts).

Row 3 and every odd-numbered row (RS): ch 1, 1 sc in each st, turn.

Row 4 (WS): ch 1, 1 sc in each of next 21 sts; using yarn C, 1 bo in next st; using yarn A, 1 sc in each of next 5 sts, turn.

Row 6 (WS): ch 1, 1 sc in each of next 18 sts; using yarn D, 1 bo in next st; using yarn A, 1 sc in each of next 5 sts; using yarn B, 1 bo in next st; using yarn A, 1 sc in each of next 2 sts, turn.

Row 8 (WS): ch 1, 1 sc in each of next 15 sts; using yarn E, 1 bo in next st; using yarn A, 1 sc in each of next 5 sts; using yarn C, 1 bo in next st; using yarn A, 1 sc in each of next 5 sts, turn.

Row 10 (WS): ch 1, 1 sc in each of next 12 sts; using yarn F, 1 bo in next st; using yarn A,

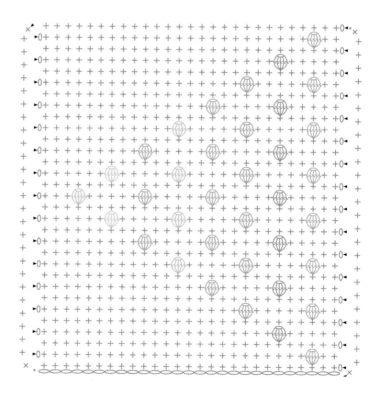

1 sc in each of next 5 sts; using **yarn D**, 1 bo in next st; using **yarn A**, 1 sc in each of next 5 sts; using **yarn B**, 1 bo in next st; using **yarn A**, 1 sc in each of next 2 sts, turn.

Row 12 (WS): ch 1, 1 sc in each of next 9 sts; using **yarn G**, 1 bo in next st; using **yarn A**, 1 sc in each of next 5 sts; using **yarn E**, 1 bo in next st; using **yarn A**, 1 sc in each of next 5 sts; using **yarn C**, 1 bo in next st; using **yarn A**, 1 sc in each of next 5 sts, turn.

Row 14 (WS): ch 1, 1 sc in each of next 6 sts; using **yarn H**, 1 bo in next st; using **yarn A**, 1 sc in each of next 5 sts; using **yarn E**, 1 bo in next st; using **yarn A**, 1 sc in each of next 5 sts; using **yarn D**, 1 bo in next st; using **yarn A**, 1 sc in each of next 5 sts; using **yarn B**, 1 bo in next st; using **yarn A**, 1 sc in each of next 2 sts, turn.

Row 16 (WS): ch 1, 1 sc in each of next 3 sts; using **yarn I**, 1 bo in next st; using **yarn A**, 1 sc in each of next 5 sts; using **yarn G**, 1 bo in next st; using **yarn A**, 1 sc in each of next 5 sts; using **yarn E**, 1 bo in next st; using **yarn A**, 1 sc in each of next 5 sts; using **yarn C**, 1 bo in next st; using **yarn A**, 1 sc in each of next 5 sts, turn.

Row 18 (WS): rep row 14.
Row 20 (WS): rep row 12.
Row 22 (WS): rep row 10.
Row 24 (WS): rep row 8.
Row 26 (WS): rep row 6.
Row 28 (WS): rep row 4.
Row 30 (WS): rep row 2.
Row 31 (RS): rep row 1.

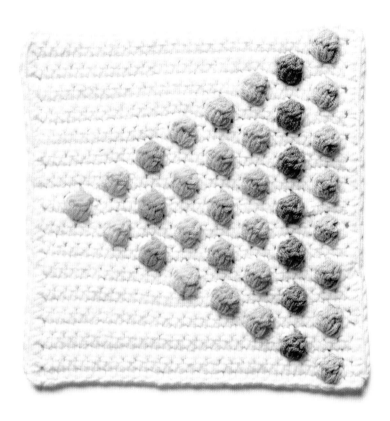

EDGING

To neaten the edges, you can work a row of sc along each rough edge.

Row 1 (RS): using **yarn A**, in left-hand top corner, do not ch 1, evenly space 27 sc along row ends, sl st in first foundation ch. Fasten off **yarn A**.

Row 2 (RS): using **yarn A**, in right-hand bottom corner in last foundation ch, do not ch 1, evenly space 27 sc along row ends, sl st in first st of top row. Fasten off **yarn A**.

Weave in ends and block.

NOTES: Use a separate piece of yarn for each bobble.

To change color when working a bobble, change color on the last yarn over when closing the stitch.

Dazzling Octagon

The brilliant colors radiating from the center of this square create a mesmerizing design.

Using **yarn A**, start with a magic ring.

Round 1 (RS): ch 1 (does not count as st throughout), 8 sc into ring, sl st in beginning sc (8 sts).

Round 2 (RS): ch 1, 2 sc in each st around, sl st in beginning sc (16 sts).

Fasten off **yarn A**.

Round 3 (RS): using **yarn B**, in any st, ch 5 (counts as 1 dc, ch 2), 1 dc in same st, skip next st, [(1 dc, ch 2, 1 dc) in next st, skip next st] seven times, sl st in third ch of beginning ch 5 (16 dc, 8 x 2-ch sp).

Fasten off **yarn B**.

Round 4 (RS): using **yarn C**, in any 2-ch sp, ch 3 (counts as 1 dc), [1 dc, ch 2, 2 dc] in same 2-ch sp, skip next 2 sts, [(2 dc, ch 2, 2 dc) in next 2-ch sp, skip next 2 sts] seven times, sl st in third ch of beginning ch 3 (32 dc, 8 x 2-ch sp).

Fasten off **yarn C**.

Round 5 (RS): using **yarn D**, in any 2-ch sp, ch 3, [1 dc, ch 2, 2 dc] in same 2-ch sp, [1 dc in next st, skip next 2 sts, 1 dc in next st, (2 dc, ch 2, 2 dc) in next 2-ch sp] eight times, omit [2 dc, ch 2, 2 dc] on last rep, sl st in third ch of beginning ch 3 (48 dc, 8 x 2-ch sp).

Fasten off **yarn D**.

Round 6 (RS): using **yarn E**, in any 2-ch sp, ch 3, [1 dc, ch 2, 2 dc] in same 2-ch sp, [1 dc in each of next 2 sts, skip next 2 sts, 1 dc in each of next 2 sts, (2 dc, ch 2, 2 dc) in next 2-ch sp] eight times, omit [2 dc, ch 2, 2 dc] on last rep, sl st in third ch of beginning ch 3 (64 dc, 8 x 2-ch sp).

Fasten off **yarn E**.

Round 7 (RS): using **yarn F**, in any 2-ch sp, ch 1, [3 sc in 2-ch sp, 1 sc in each of next 3 sts, sc2tog over next 2 sts, 1 sc in each of next 3 sts] eight times, sl st in beginning sc (80 sts).

Fasten off **yarn F**.

Round 8 (RS): using **yarn G**, in second sc of any 3 sc group, ch 4 (counts as 1 tr), [1 tr, ch 2, 2 tr] in same st, [1 dc in each of next 5 sts, 1 hdc in next st, 1 sc in next st, 1 sl st in each of next 5 sts, 1 sc in next st, 1 hdc in next st, 1 dc in each of next 5 sts, (2 tr, ch 2, 2 tr) in next st] four times, omit [2 tr, ch 2, 2 tr] on last rep, sl st in fourth ch of beginning ch 4 (92 sts, 4 x 2-ch sp).

Fasten off **yarn G**.

Round 9 (RS): using **yarn H**, in any 2-ch sp, ch 4 (counts as 1 hdc, ch 2), 1 hdc in same 2-ch sp, [1 hdc in each of next 9 sts, 1 sc in each of next 5 sl st, 1 hdc in each of next

<table>
</table>

SKILL LEVEL

HOOK SIZE	BLOCK SIZE
US E/4 (3.5mm)	6 x 6in (15 x 15cm)

YARN/COLORS

Sample uses Scheepjes Softfun

A = Orchid (#2657)

B = Heath (#2493)

C = Bright Turquoise (#2423)

D = Botanical (#2615)

E = Mint (#2640)

F = Canary (#2518)

G = Cantaloupe (#2652)

H = Magenta (#2654)

I = Rose (#2514)

J = Light Rose (#2513)

STITCHES

ch—chain

sl st—slip stitch

sc—single crochet

hdc—half double crochet

dc—double crochet

tr—treble crochet

sc2tog—single crochet 2 sts together

MIX AND MATCH

Page 14   +   Page 60

CHART KEY

For symbol key, see page 122

9 sts, (1 hdc, ch 2, 1 hdc) in next 2-ch sp] four times, omit [1 hdc, ch 2, 1 hdc] on last rep, sl st in second ch of beginning ch 4 (100 sts, 4 x 2-ch sp).

Fasten off **yarn H**.

Round 10 (RS): using **yarn I**, in any 2-ch sp, ch 3, [1 dc, ch 2, 2 dc] in same 2-ch sp, [1 dc in each of next 2 sts, ch 1, skip next st, (1 dc in each of next 4 sts, ch 1, skip next st) four times, 1 dc in each of next 2 sts, (2 dc, ch 2, 2 dc] in next 2-ch sp] four times, omit [2 dc, ch 2, 2 dc] on last rep, sl st in third ch of beginning ch 3 (96 dc, 4 x 2-ch sp, 20 x ch sp).

Fasten off **yarn I**.

Round 11 (RS): using **yarn J**, in any 2-ch sp, ch 4, 1 hdc in same 2-ch sp, 1 hdc in each of next 4 sts, [(ch 1, skip next ch sp, 1 hdc in each of next 4 sts) five times, (1 hdc, ch 2, 1 hdc) in next 2-ch sp] four times, omit [1 hdc, ch 2, 1 hdc] on last rep, sl st in second ch of beginning ch 4. (104 hdc, 4 x 2-ch sp, 20 x ch sp).

Fasten off **yarn J**.

Weave in ends and block.

SKILL LEVEL

HOOK SIZE	BLOCK SIZE
US E/4 (3.5mm)	6 x 6in (15 x 15cm)

TECHNIQUES

Working over/into previous rounds/rows
(see page 119)

YARN/COLORS

Sample uses Scheepjes Softfun

A = Canary (#2518)	F = Deep Violet
B = Cantaloupe	(#2515)
(#2652)	G = Cool Blue (#2603)
C = Hot Pink (#2495)	H = Apple (#2516)
D = Light Rose (#2513)	I = Green Tea (#2639)
E = Orchid (#2657)	

STITCHES

ch—chain	tr—treble crochet
sl st—slip stitch	sc2tog—single crochet
sc—single crochet	2 sts together
hdc—half double	dc3tog—double
crochet	crochet 3 sts together
dc—double crochet	

MIX AND MATCH

Page 30 + Page 50 + Page 86

CHART KEY

For symbol key, see page 122

Pop Flower

Work this square in different colors to make your project pop.

Using **yarn A**, start with a magic ring.

Round 1 (RS): ch 3 (counts as 1 dc), 11 dc into ring, sl st in second ch of beginning ch 2 (12 sts).

Round 2 (RS): ch 1 (does not count as st), [2 sc in next st, 1 sc in next st] six times, sl st in beginning ch (18 sts).

Fasten off **yarn A**.

Round 3 (RS): using **yarn B**, [1 sl st, ch 2, 1 dc, 1 tr] in any st, [(1 tr, 1 dc, ch 2, 1 sl st) in next st, ch 1, skip next st, (1 sl st, ch 2, 1 dc, 1 tr) in next st] six times, omit [1 sl st, ch 2, 1 dc, 1 tr] on last rep, sl st in beginning sl st (6 petals, 6 x ch sp).

Fasten off **yarn B**.

NOTE: For the next round, most stitches are worked into round 3. Work over round 3 ch sp when instructed to work into round 2.

Round 4 (RS): using **yarn C**, sl st in any skipped round 2 st, [1 sc in next 2-ch sp,

1 hdc in next st, 4 dc in each of next 2 sts, 1 hdc in next st, 1 sc in next 2-ch sp, 1 sl st in next skipped round 2 st] six times, omit 1 sl st on last rep, sl st in beginning sl st (78 sts).
Fasten off **yarn C**.

Round 5 (RS): using **yarn D**, in fourth dc of any group of 8 dc, ch 2 (counts as 1 hdc), 2 hdc in same st, [2 hdc in next st, 1 hdc in each of next 3 sts, sc2tog over next 2 hdc, 1 hdc in each of next 3 sts, 3 hdc in next st] six times, omit 3 hdc on last rep, sl st in second ch of beginning ch 2 (72 sts).
Fasten off **yarn D**.

Round 6 (RS): using **yarn E**, sl st in any third hdc of any 3 hdc group, [1 sc in each of next 2 sts, 1 hdc in next st, 1 dc in next st, dc3tog over next 3 sts, 1 dc in next st, 1 hdc in next st, 1 sc in each of next 2 sts, 1 sl st in next st] six times, omit 1 sl st on last rep, sl st in beginning sl st (60 sts).
Fasten off **yarn E**.

Round 7 (RS): using **yarn F**, in any dc3tog, ch 1, 1 sc in same st, [ch 3, skip next 2 sts, 1 sc in next st] twenty times, omit 1 sc on last rep, sl st in beginning sc (20 sc, 20 x 3-ch sp).
Fasten off **yarn F**.

Round 8 (RS): using **yarn G**, in any 3-ch sp, ch 4 (counts as 1 tr), [2 tr, ch 3, 3 tr] in same 3-ch sp, [ch 1, skip next st, 3 dc in next 3-ch sp, ch 1, skip next st, (1 dc, 2 hdc) in next 3-ch sp, ch 1, skip next st, (2 hdc, 1 dc) in next 3-ch sp, ch 1, skip next st, 3 dc in next 3-ch sp, ch 1, skip next st, (3 tr, ch 3, 3 tr) in next 3-ch sp] four times, omit [3 tr, ch 3, 3 tr] on

last rep, sl st in fourth ch of beginning ch 4 (72 sts, 4 x 3-ch sp, 20 x ch sp).
Fasten off **yarn G**.

Round 9 (RS): using **yarn H**, in any 3-ch sp, ch 3, [2 dc, ch 2, 3 dc] in same 3-ch sp, [ch 1, skip next 3 sts, (3 dc in next ch sp, ch 1, skip next 3 sts) five times, (3 dc, ch 2, 3 dc) in next 2-ch sp] four times, omit [3 dc, ch 2, 3 dc] on last rep, sl st in third ch of beginning ch 3 (84 sts, 4 x 2-ch sp, 24 x ch sp).
Fasten off **yarn H**.

Round 10 (RS): using **yarn I**, in any 2-ch sp, ch 3, [2 dc, ch 2, 3 dc] in same 2-ch sp, [ch 1, skip next 3 sts, (3 dc in next ch sp, ch 1, skip next 3 sts) six times, (3 dc, ch 2, 3 dc) in next 2-ch sp] four times, omit [3 dc, ch 2, 3 dc] on last rep, sl st in third ch of beginning ch 3 (96 sts, 4 x 2-ch sp, 28 x ch sp).
Fasten off **yarn I**.

Weave in ends and block.

HOOK SIZE	BLOCK SIZE
US G/6 (4mm)	6 x 6in (15 x 15cm)

TECHNIQUES
Working over/into previous rounds/rows
(see page 119)

YARN/COLORS
Sample uses Scheepjes Softfun

A = Rose (#2514)   E = Mint (#2640)

B = Light Rose (#2513)   F = Botanical (#2615)

C = Cantaloupe   G = Cool Blue (#2603)
(#2652)
                    H = Orchid (#2657)
D = Canary (#2518)
                    I = Snow (#2412)

STITCHES
ch—chain

sl st—slip stitch

sc—single crochet

hdc—half double crochet

dc—double crochet

tr—treble crochet

tr-2-cl—cluster made of treble crochet
2 sts together

ps—5 hdc puff stitch

MIX AND MATCH

Page 20 ➕ Page 86

CHART KEY
For symbol key, see page 122

Crocheted Flower Net
The chain spaces create a beautifully intricate fabric.

Using **yarn A**, start with a magic ring.

Round 1 (RS): ch 1 (does not count as st throughout), 8 sc into ring, sl st in beginning sc (8 sts).

Round 2 (RS): [ch 2, 1 ps in next st, ch 2, 1 sl st in next st] four times (4 ps, 8 x 2-ch sp, 4 sl st). Fasten off **yarn A**.

NOTE: For the next round, work 3 dc group over round 2 sl st and into round 1 st.

Round 3 (RS): using **yarn B**, in any ps, ch 1, [1 sc in ps, ch 1, 3 dc in round 1 st below, ch 1] four times, sl st in beginning sc (12 dc, 4 sc, 8 x ch sp).

Fasten off **yarn B**.

Round 4 (RS): using **yarn C**, in second dc of any 3 dc group, [1 sl st in second dc of 3 dc group, skip next st, skip next ch sp, (tr-2-cl, ch 4, 1 sc, ch 4, tr-2-cl) in next st, skip next

ch sp, skip next st] four times, sl st in beginning sl st (8 tr-cl, 4 sl st, 4 sc, 8 × 4-ch sp).

Fasten off **yarn C.**

NOTE: For the next round, work all ps over round 4 sl st and into round 3 st.

Round 5 (RS): using **yarn D,** in first 4-ch sp made in round 4, ch 1, [(1 sc, 1 hdc, 1 dc, 1 tr) in 4-ch sp, ch 2, skip next sc, (1 tr, 1 dc, 1 hdc, 1 sc) in next 4-ch sp, ch 1, skip next tr-2-cl, 1 ps in second dc of 3 dc group of round 3 below, ch 1, skip next tr-2-cl] four times, sl st in beginning sc (8 tr, 8 dc, 8 hdc, 8 sc, 4 ps, 8 × ch sp, 4 × 2-ch sp).

Fasten off **yarn D.**

Round 6 (RS): using **yarn E,** in any 2-ch sp, [(1 sl st, ch 5, 1 sl st) in 2-ch sp, (ch 2, skip next st, 1 sl st in next st) twice, ch 2, skip next ch sp, 1 sl st in next ps, ch 2, skip next ch sp, (1 sl st in next st, ch 2, skip next st) twice] four times, sl st in beginning sl st (24 × 2-ch sp, 4 × 5-ch sp).

Fasten off **yarn E.**

Round 7 (RS): using **yarn F,** in any 5-ch sp, ch 1, [1 sc in 5-ch sp, ch 3, (1 sl st in next 2-ch sp, ch 3) six times] four times, sl st in beginning sc (28 × 3-ch sp, 4 sc).

Fasten off **yarn F.**

Round 8 (RS): using **yarn G,** in 3-ch sp right of any sc, ch 3 (counts as 1 dc), 2 dc in same 3-ch sp, ch 2, [3 dc in next 3-ch sp, ch 2, (1 dc in next 3-ch sp, ch 2) five times, 3 dc in next 3-ch sp, ch 2] four times, omit [3 dc in next 3-ch sp, ch 2] on last rep, sl st in third ch of beginning ch 3 (48 dc, 24 × 2-ch sp).

Fasten off **yarn G.**

Round 9 (RS): using **yarn H,** in any corner 2-ch sp, ch 6 (counts as 1 dc, ch 3), 1 dc in same st, [ch 2, skip next 2 sts, (1 dc in next st, ch 2, skip next 2-ch sp) twice, (1 ps in next st,

ch 2, skip next 2-ch sp) three times, 1 dc in next st, ch 2, skip next 2-ch sp, 1 dc in next st, ch 2, skip next 2 sts, (1 dc, ch 3, 1 dc) in next st] four times, omit [1 dc, ch 3, 1 dc] on last rep, sl st in third ch of beginning ch 6 (24 dc, 12 ps, 32 × 2-ch sp, 4 × 3-ch sp).

Fasten off **yarn H.**

Round 10 (RS): using **yarn A,** in any 3-ch sp, ch 3, [2 dc, ch 2, 3 dc] in same 3-ch sp, [ch 2, skip next st, skip next 2-ch sp, (1 dc in next st, ch 2, skip next 2-ch sp) seven times, skip next st, (3 dc, ch 2, 3 dc) in next 3-ch sp] four times, omit [3 dc, ch 2, 3 dc] on last rep, sl st in third ch of beginning ch 3 (52 dc, 36 × 2-ch sp).

Fasten off **yarn A.**

Round 11 (RS): using **yarn I,** in any corner 2-ch sp, ch 1, [(1 sc, ch 2, 1 sc) in 2-ch sp, 1 sc in each of next 3 sts, (2 sc in next 2-ch sp, 1 sc in next st) twice, (1 sc in next 2-ch sp, 1 sc in next st) four times, (2 sc in next 2-ch sp, 1 sc in next st) twice, 1 sc in each of next 2 sts] four times, omit [1 sc, ch 2, 1 sc] on last rep, sl st in third ch of beginning ch 3 (108 sts, 4 × 2-ch sp).

Fasten off **yarn I.**

Weave in ends and block.

HOOK SIZE	BLOCK SIZE
US G/6 (4mm)	6 x 6in (15 x 15cm)

TECHNIQUES

Changing color on row/round (see page 121)

Working into round/row ends (see page 125)

Working with multiple colors at the same time/
tapestry crochet (see page 121)

YARN/COLORS

Sample uses Scheepjes Softfun

A = Botanical (#2615)

B = Orchid (#2657)

C = Butterscotch (#2610)

D = Rose (#2514)

E = Cool Blue (#2603)

F = Snow (#2412)

STITCHES

ch—chain

sl st—slip stitch

sc—single crochet

lp—loop stitch (see notes at end of pattern)

MIX AND MATCH

Page 50 ✛ Page 30

CHART KEY

For symbol key, see page 122

Loop and Twist

The loop and single crochet stitches create a fabulous texture.

Using yarn A, ch 31.

Row 1 (RS): 1 sc in second ch from hook, 1 sc in each ch across, turn (30 sts).

Row 2 (WS): ch 1 (does not count as st throughout), 1 sc in each st, turn (30 sts).

Row 3 (RS): ch 1, 1 sc in each of next 23 sts; using yarn B, 1 sc in each of next 6 sts; using yarn A, 1 sc in next st; using yarn B, turn (30 sts).

Row 4 (WS): ch 1, 1 lp st in each of next 11 sts; using yarn A, 1 sc in each of next 19 sts, turn (30 sts).

Row 5 (RS): ch 1, 1 sc in each of next 17 sts; using yarn B, 1 sc in each of next 13 sts, turn (30 sts).

Row 6 (WS): ch 1, 1 lp st in each of next 14 sts; using yarn A, 1 sc in each of next 16 sts; using yarn B, turn (30 sts).

Row 7 (RS): ch 1, 1 sc in each of next 3 sts; using yarn A, 1 sc in each of next 11 sts; using yarn B, 1 sc in each of next 12 sts; using yarn C, 1 sc in each of next 4 sts, turn (30 sts).

Row 8 (WS): ch 1, 1 sc in each of next 5 sts; using yarn B, 1 lp st in each of next 12 sts;

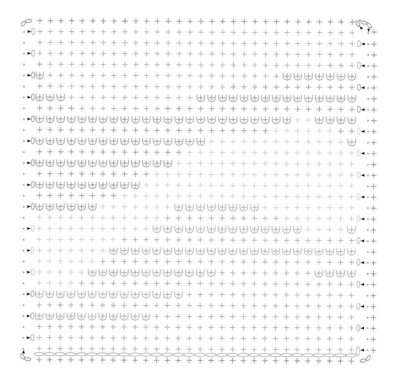

using yarn A, 1 sc in each of next 9 sts; using yarn B, 1 lp st in each of next 4 sts, turn (30 sts).

Row 9 (RS): ch 1, 1 sc in each of next 5 sts; using yarn A, 1 sc in each of next 6 sts; using yarn B, 1 sc in each of next 13 sts; using yarn C, 1 sc in each of next 6 sts, turn (30 sts). Fasten off yarn A.

Row 10 (WS): ch 1, 1 sc in each of next 7 sts; using yarn B, 1 lp st in each of next 23 sts, turn (30 sts).

Row 11 (RS): ch 1, 1 sc in each of next 22 sts; using yarn C, 1 sc in each of next 8 sts, turn (30 sts).

Row 12 (WS): ch 1, 1 sc in each of next 11 sts; using yarn B, 1 lp st in each of next 14 sts; using yarn C, 1 sc in each of next 4 sts; using yarn B, 1 lp st in next st; using yarn C, turn (30 sts).

Row 13 (RS): ch 1, 1 sc in each of next 7 sts; using yarn B, 1 sc in each of next 11 sts; using yarn C, 1 sc in each of next 12 sts; using yarn D, turn (30 sts).

Row 14 (WS): ch 1, 1 lp st in each of next 6 sts; using yarn C, 1 sc in each of next 7 sts; using yarn B, 1 lp st in each of next 8 sts; using yarn C, 1 sc in each of next 9 sts, turn (30 sts).

Fasten off yarn B.

Row 15 (RS): ch 1, 1 sc in each of next 22 sts; using yarn D, 1 sc in each of next 8 sts, turn (30 sts).

Row 16 (WS): ch 1, 1 lp st in each of next 10 sts; using yarn C, 1 sc in each of next 20 sts, turn (30 sts).

Row 17 (RS): ch 1, 1 sc in each of next 19 sts; using yarn D, 1 sc in each of next 11 sts, turn (30 sts).

Row 18 (WS): ch 1, 1 lp st in each of next 13 sts; using yarn C, 1 sc in each of next 17 sts, turn (30 sts).

Row 19 (RS): ch 1, 1 sc in each of next 16 sts; using yarn D, 1 sc in each of next 14 sts, turn (30 sts).

Row 20 (WS): ch 1, 1 lp st in each of next 16 sts; using yarn C, 1 sc in each of next 13 sts; using yarn D, 1 lp st in next st, turn (30 sts).

Row 21 (RS): ch 1, 1 sc in each of next 2 sts; using yarn C, 1 sc in each of next 6 sts; using yarn D, 1 sc in each of next 22 sts, turn (30 sts).

Row 22 (WS): ch 1, 1 lp st in each of next 24 sts; using yarn C, 1 sc in each of next 2 sts; using yarn D, 1 lp st in each of next 4 sts, turn (30 sts).

Fasten off yarn C.

Row 23 (RS): ch 1, 1 sc in each of next 18 sts; using yarn E, 1 sc in each of next 8 sts; using yarn D, 1 sc in each of next 4 sts, turn (30 sts).

Row 24 (WS): ch 1, 1 lp st in each of next 3 sts; using yarn E, 1 sc in each of next 12 sts; using yarn D, 1 lp st in each of next 15 sts, turn (30 sts).

Row 25 (RS): ch 1, 1 sc in each of next 12 sts; using yarn E, 1 sc in each of next 16 sts; using yarn D, 1 sc in each of next 2 sts, turn (30 sts).

Row 26 (WS): ch 1, 1 lp st in next st; using yarn E, 1 sc in each of next 22 sts; using yarn D, 1 lp st in each of next 7 sts; using yarn E, turn (30 sts).

Row 27 (RS): ch 1, 1 sc in next st; using yarn D, 1 sc in each of next 2 sts; using yarn E, 1 sc in each of next 26 sts; using yarn D, 1 sc in next st; using yarn E, turn (30 sts).

Fasten off yarn D.

Row 28 (WS): rep row 2 using yarn E (30 sts).
Row 29 (RS): rep row 28 (30 sts).
Row 30 (WS): rep row 28 (30 sts).
Fasten off yarn E.

BORDER

To create a border that is as neat as possible, (RS): using yarn F, evenly space 30 sl st along one of the vertical edges of work, fasten off, and repeat on the opposite side. Fasten off yarn F.

Round 1 (RS): using yarn F, in last st of row 30, ch 1, [1 sc in each of next 30 sc, ch 2, 1 sc in each of next 30 sl st, ch 2] twice, sl st in beginning sc (120 sts).

Fasten off yarn F.

Weave in ends and block.

NOTES: Loop stitches are only made on wrong side (WS) rows.

To work loop stitch, wrap yarn over index finger of your yarn hand and insert hook into stitch, bring your hook over the yarn, keeping your finger in place. Grab the strand of yarn from behind your index finger, also catching the other strand of yarn that you passed your hook over before, and pull both through the stitch. You should now have three loops on your hook, and a loop of yarn wrapped around your index finger. Pull your working yarn until the loop is at your desired size. Yarn over and pull through all three of the loops on your hook.

Watermelon Slice

You'll need to make more than one of these juicy squares.

Using yarn A, ch 3.

Row 1 (WS): 3 dc in third ch from hook, turn (3 sts).

Row 2 (RS): ch 2 (does not count as st throughout), 2 dc in each st, turn (6 sts).

Row 3 (WS): ch 2, [2 dc in next st, 1 dc in next st] three times, turn (9 sts).

Row 4 (RS): ch 2, [2 dc in next st, 1 dc in each of next 2 sts] three times, turn (12 sts).

Row 5 (WS): ch 2, [2 dc in next st, 1 dc in each of next 3 sts] three times, turn (15 sts).

Row 6 (RS): ch 2, 2 dc in next st, 1 dc in each of next 2 sts; using yarn B, 1 ps in next st; using yarn A, 1 dc in next st, 2 dc in next st; using yarn B, 1 ps in next st; using yarn A, 1 dc in each of next 3 sts; using yarn B, 1 ps in next st; using yarn A, 1 dc in same st, 1 dc in each of next 4 sts, turn (18 sts).

Row 7 (WS): ch 2, [2 dc in next st, 1 dc in each of next 5 sts] three times, turn (21 sts).

Row 8 (RS): ch 2, 2 dc in next st, 1 dc in each of next 2 sts; using yarn B, 1 ps in next st;

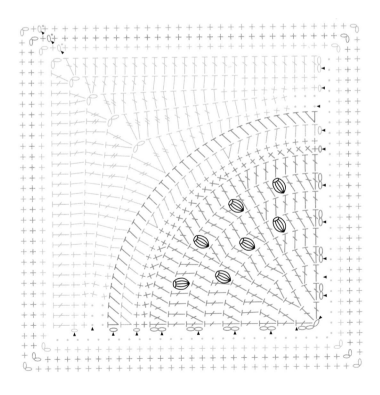

SKILL LEVEL

HOOK SIZE	BLOCK SIZE
US E/4 (3.5mm)	6 x 6in (15 x 15cm)

TECHNIQUES
Changing color on row/round (see page 121)
Working into round/row ends (see page 125)
Working with multiple colors at the same time/
tapestry crochet (see page 121)

YARN/COLORS
Sample uses Scheepjes Softfun

A = Coral (#2607)	D = Apple (#2516)
B = Black (#2408)	E = Emerald (#2605)
C = Snow (#2412)	F = Light Rose (#2513)

STITCHES

ch—chain	dc—double crochet
sl st—slip stitch	tr—treble crochet
sc—single crochet	ps—5 hdc puff stitch
hdc—half double crochet	

MIX AND MATCH

Page 12 + Page 38

CHART KEY
For symbol key, see page 122

using yarn A, 1 dc in each of next 3 sts, 1 dc in next st; using yarn B, 1 ps in same st; using yarn A, 1 dc in each of next 4 sts; using yarn B, 1 ps in next st; using yarn A, 1 dc in next st, 2 dc in next st, 1 dc in next st; using yarn B, 1 ps in next st; using yarn A, 1 dc in each of next 4 sts, turn (24 sts).

Fasten off yarn B.

Row 9 (WS): ch 2, [2 dc in next st, 1 dc in each of next 7 sts] three times, turn (27 sts).

Row 10 (RS): ch 1 (does not count as st throughout), [2 sc in next st, 1 sc in each of next 8 sts] three times, join yarn C, turn (30 sts).

Fasten off yarn A.

Row 11 (WS): ch 1, 1 sc in each st, join yarn D, turn (30 sts).

Fasten off yarn C.

Row 12 (RS): ch 1, [1 hdc in each of next 9 sts, 2 hdc in next st] three times, join yarn E, turn (33 sts).

Fasten off yarn D.

Row 13 (WS): ch 1, 2 hdc in next st, 1 hdc in each of next 31 sts, 2 hdc in next st, join yarn F, turn (35 sts).

Fasten off yarn E.

Row 14 (RS): 1 sl st in each of next 3 sts, 1 sc in each of next 5 sts, 1 hdc in each of next 4 sts, 1 dc in each of next 4 sts, 1 tr in next st, [1 tr, ch 2, 1 tr] in next st, 1 tr in next st, 1 dc in each of next 4 sts, 1 hdc in each of next 4 sts, 1 sc in each of next 5 sts, 1 sl st in each of next 3 sts, turn (36 sts).

Row 15 (WS): 1 sl st in each of next 3 sts, 1 sc in each of next 3 sts, 1 hdc in each of next 5 sts, 1 dc in each of next 4 sts, 1 tr in each of next 3 sts, [2 tr, ch 2, 2 tr] in next 2-ch sp, 1 tr in each of next 3 sts, 1 dc in each of next 4 sts, 1 hdc in each of next 5 sts, 1 sc in each of next 3 sts, 1 sl st in each of next 3 sts, turn (40 sts).

Row 16 (RS): ch 1, 1 sc in each of next 10 sts, 1 hdc in each of next 5 sts, 1 dc in each of next 5 sts, [2 tr, ch 2, 2 tr] in next 2-ch sp, 1 dc in each of next 5 sts, 1 hdc in each of next 5 sts, 1 sc in each of next 10 sts, turn (44 sts).

Row 17 (WS): ch 1, 1 sc in each of next 8 sts, 1 hdc in each of next 9 sts, 1 dc in each of next 5 sts, [2 dc, ch 2, 2 dc] in next 2-ch sp, 1 dc in each of next 5 sts, 1 hdc in each of next 9 sts, 1 sc in each of next 8 sts, turn (48 sts).

Row 18 (RS): ch 2, 1 dc in each of next 24 sts, [2 dc, ch 2, 2 dc] in next 2-ch sp, 1 dc in each of next 24 sts (52 sts).

Fasten off yarn F.

BORDER

To create a border that is as neat as possible, (RS): using yarn F, evenly space 27 sl st along one of the raw edges of work, fasten off, and repeat on the remaining edge.

Fasten off yarn F.

Round 1 (RS): using yarn F, in 2-ch sp of row 18, ch 1, [1 sc, ch 2, 1 sc] in same 2-ch sp, 1 sc in each of next 26 sts, ch 2, [1 sc in each of next 27 sl st, ch 2] twice, 1 sc in each of next 26 sts, sl st in beginning sc (108 sts).

Fasten off yarn F.

Round 2 (RS): using yarn C, in any 2-ch sp, ch 1, [[1 sc, ch 2, 1 sc] in 2-ch sp, 1 sc in each of next 27 sts] four times, sl st in beginning sc (116 sts).

Fasten off yarn C.

Round 3 (RS): using yarn D, in any 2-ch sp, ch 1, [[1 sc, ch 2, 1 sc] in 2-ch sp, 1 sc in each of next 29 sts] four times, sl st in beginning sc (124 sts).

Fasten off yarn D.

Weave in ends and block.

NOTES: Do not fasten off any colors until instructed.
Puff stitches are made on the right side (RS).

Rainbow Arch

See page 104 for how to make a gorgeous wall hanging based on this square.

Using yarn A, ch 14.

Row 1 (WS): 1 hdc in third ch from hook (skipped 2 ch count as 1 hdc), 1 hdc in each of next 10 ch, 6 hdc in next ch; working into other side of foundation ch, 1 hdc in each of next 12 ch, turn (30 sts).

Row 2 (RS): ch 2 (does not count as st throughout), 1 dc in each of next 12 sts, 2 dc in each of next 6 sts, 1 dc in each of next 12 sts, join yarn B, turn (36 sts).

Fasten off yarn A.

Row 3 (WS): ch 2, 1 dc in each of next 12 sts, [2 dc in next st, 1 dc in next st] six times, 1 dc in each st until end, join yarn C, turn (42 sts).

Fasten off yarn B.

Row 4 (RS): ch 2, 1 dc in each of next 12 sts, [2 dc in next st, 1 dc in each of next 2 sts] six times, 1 dc in each st until end, join yarn D, turn (48 sts).

Fasten off yarn C.

Row 5 (WS): ch 1 (does not count as st throughout), 1 hdc in each of next 12 sts, [2 hdc in next st, 1 hdc in each of next 3 sts] six times, 1 hdc in each st until end, join yarn E, turn (54 sts).

Fasten off yarn D.

Row 6 (RS): ch 2, 1 dc in each of next 12 sts, [2 dc in next st, 1 dc in each of next 4 sts] six times, 1 dc in each st until end, join yarn F, turn (60 sts).

Fasten off yarn E.

Row 7 (WS): ch 1, 1 hdc in each of next 12 sts, [2 hdc in next st, 1 hdc in each of next 5 sts] six times, 1 hdc in each st until end, join yarn G, turn (66 sts).

Fasten off yarn F.

Row 8 (RS): ch 1, 1 hdc in each of next 12 sts, [2 hdc in next st, 1 hdc in each of next 6 sts] six times, 1 hdc in each st until end, join yarn H, turn (72 sts).

Fasten off yarn G.

Row 9 (WS): ch 1, 1 sc in each st until end, join yarn A, turn (72 sts).

Fasten off yarn H.

BORDER

Round 1 (RS): 1 sl st in each of next 17 sts, 1 sc in each of next 2 sts, 1 hdc in each of next 2 sts, 1 dc in each of next 2 sts, [2 tr, 1 dtr] in next st, ch 2, 2 dtr in next st, 1 tr in each of next 2 sts, 1 dc in each of next 3 sts, 1 hdc in each of next 2 sts, 1 sc in each of next 8 sts, 1 hdc in each of next 2 sts, 1 dc in each of next 3 sts, 1 tr in each of next 2 sts,

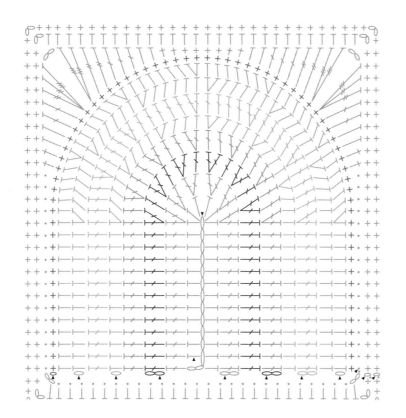

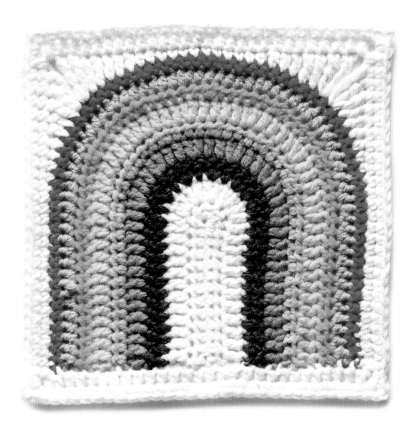

HOOK SIZE	BLOCK SIZE
US E/4 (3.5mm)	6 x 6in (15 x 15cm)

TECHNIQUES
Changing color on row/round (see page 121)
Working into round/row ends (see page 125)

YARN/COLORS
Sample uses Scheepjes Softfun

A = Snow (#2412)   D = Apple (#2516)
B = Deep Violet   E = Canary (#2518)
(#2515)   F = Tangerine (#2427)
C = Bright Turquoise   G = Rose (#2514)
(#2423)   H = Magenta (#2654)

STITCHES
ch—chain
sl st—slip stitch
sc—single crochet
hdc—half double crochet
dc—double crochet
tr—treble crochet
dtr—double treble crochet

MIX AND MATCH

Page 28 + Page 50

CHART KEY
For symbol key, see page 122

2 dtr in next st, ch 2, [1 dtr, 2 tr] in next st, 1 dc in each of next 2 sts, 1 hdc in each of next 2 sts, 1 sc in each of next 2 sts, 1 sl st in each of next 17 sts, ch 2, evenly space 26 sl st along raw edge, ch 2, sl st in beginning sl st (104 sts).

Round 2 (RS): ch 1, [1 sc in each of next 26 sts, (1 sc, ch 2, 1 hdc) in next 2-ch sp, 1 hdc in each of next 26 sts, (1 hdc, ch 2, 1 sc) in next 2-ch sp] twice, sl st in beginning sc (112 sts).

Round 3 (RS): ch 1, 1 sc in each of next 27 sts, [(1 sc, ch 2, 1 sc) in next 2-ch sp, 1 sc in each of next 28 sts] three times, [1 sc, ch 2, 1 sc] in next 2-ch sp, 1 sc in next st, sl st in beginning sc (120 sts).

Fasten off **yarn A**.

Weave in ends and block.

NOTE: While not crucial, blocking the center rainbow motif before moving on to the border is recommended to assist with shaping.

Stripe Color Block

This block alternates contrasting colors to create a striking look.

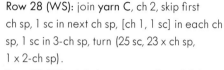

Using yarn A, ch 3.

Row 1 (RS): 1 sc in third ch from hook, turn.

Row 2 (WS): ch 3, [1 sc, ch 1, 1 sc] in 2-ch sp, turn.

Row 3 (RS): ch 3, 1 sc in next ch sp, ch 1, [1 sc, ch 1, 1 sc] in 3-ch sp, fasten off yarn A, turn.

Row 4 (WS): join yarn B, ch 3, [1 sc, ch 1] in each ch sp, [1 sc, ch 1, 1 sc] in 3-ch sp, fasten off yarn B, turn.

Row 5 (RS): rep row 4 using yarn C, fasten off yarn C, turn.

Row 6 (WS): rep row 4 using yarn B, fasten off yarn B, turn.

Rows 7–9: rep row 4 using yarn A, fasten off yarn A at end of row 9, turn.

Rows 10–27: rep rows 4–9 three times, fasten off yarn A at end of row 27, turn (27 sc, 26 x ch sp, 1 x 3-ch sp).

Row 28 (WS): join yarn C, ch 2, skip first ch sp, 1 sc in next ch sp, [ch 1, 1 sc] in each ch sp, 1 sc in 3-ch sp, turn (25 sc, 23 x ch sp, 1 x 2-ch sp).

Row 29 (RS): ch 2, 1 sc in next ch sp, [ch 1, 1 sc] in each ch sp, 1 sc in 2-ch sp, turn (24 sc, 22 x ch sp, 1 x 2-ch sp).

Rows 30–50: rep row 29 (3 sc, 1 x ch sp, 1 x 2-ch sp).

Row 51 (RS): ch 2, 1 sc in ch sp, 1 sc in ch 2, turn.

Row 52 (WS): ch 2, 1 sc in 2-ch sp, turn (1 sc, 1 x 2-ch sp).

Row 53 (RS): ch 1, 1 sc in 2-ch sp, fasten off yarn C (1 sc).

EDGING (OPTIONAL)

Round 1 (RS): join yarn C in side of row 28 beginning ch 2, ch 1 (does not count as st), 2 sc in same place, 1 sc in side of each row across, 1 sc in corner, turn 90 degrees, 1 sc in each row across, fasten off yarn C and change to yarn A, [1 sc in corner, turn 90 degrees, 1 sc in side of each row across] twice, sl st in beginning sc, fasten off yarn A (112 sts).

NOTE: The majority of this square is worked in chain spaces. Skip single crochet stitches unless otherwise instructed.

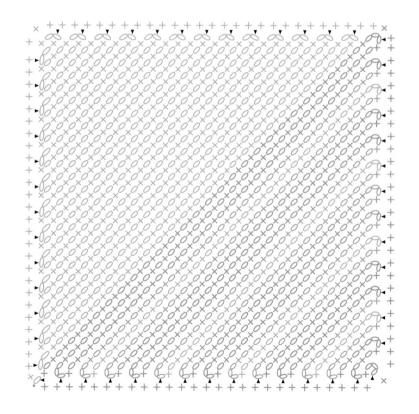

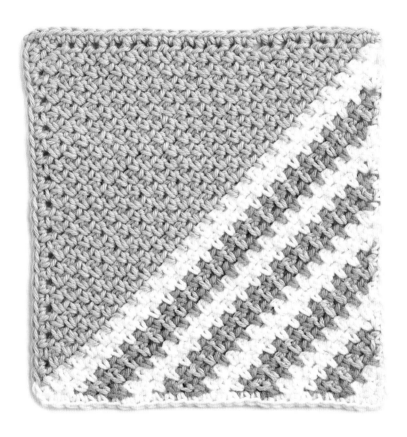

SKILL LEVEL

HOOK SIZE	BLOCK SIZE
US G/6 (4mm)	6 x 6in (15 x 15cm)

TECHNIQUES
Changing color on row/round (see page 121)
Working into round/row ends (see page 125)

YARN/COLORS
Sample uses Paintbox Cotton DK
A = Paper White (#401)
B = Bubblegum Pink (#451)
C = Marine Blue (#434)

STITCHES
ch—chain
sl st—slip stitch
sc—single crochet

MIX AND MATCH

  +

Page 58   +   Page 38

CHART KEY
For symbol key, see page 122

HOOK SIZE	BLOCK SIZE
US G/6 (4mm) and US C/2 (3mm)	6 x 6in (15 x 15cm)

TECHNIQUES

Stitching pieces onto square (see page 98)

Adding embroidery details (see page 98)

YARN/COLORS

Sample uses Scheepjes Softfun

A = Latte (#2622)

B = Starfish (#2620)

C = Light Rose (#2513)

D = Soft Mauve (#2470)

E = Cantaloupe (#2652)

F = Dove (#2510)

STITCHES

ch—chain

sl st—slip stitch

sc—single crochet

hdc—half double crochet

dc—double crochet

tr—treble crochet

MIX AND MATCH

Page 76 ✛ Page 34

CHART KEY

For symbol key, see page 122

Cute Kitten

Use scraps of embroidery floss (thread) to add feline features.

———

Using **yarn A**, start with a magic ring.

Round 1 (RS): ch 3 (counts as 1 dc throughout), 11 dc into ring, sl st in third ch of beginning ch 3 (12 sts).

Round 2 (RS): ch 3, 1 dc in same st, 2 dc in each st around, sl st in third ch of beginning ch 3 (24 sts).

Round 3 (RS): ch 3, 1 dc in same st, 1 dc in next st, [2 dc in next st, 1 dc in next st] in each st around, sl st in third ch of beginning ch 3 (36 sts).

Round 4 (RS): ch 1 (does not count as st), 1 sc in same st, [1 sc in each of next 9 sts, 1 hdc in next st, 1 dc in each of next 6 sts, 1 hdc in next st, 1 sc in next st] twice, omit final 1 sc on last rep, sl st in beginning ch (36 sts).

Fasten off **yarn A**.

Work next round in back loops only.

Round 5 (RS): using **yarn B**, in first st made in round 4, ch 3, [1 tr, ch 2, 1 tr, 1 dc] in same st, [1 dc in next st, 1 hdc in next st, 1 sc in each

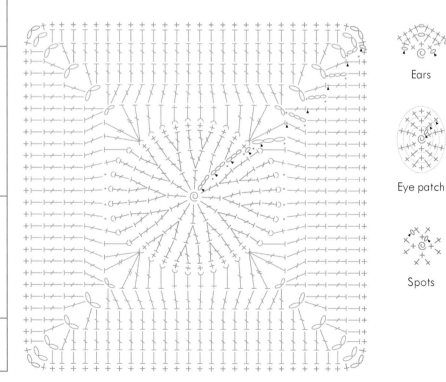

Ears

Eye patch

Spots

of next 4 sts, 1 hdc in next st, 1 dc in next st, (1 dc, 1 tr, ch 2, 1 tr, 1 dc) in next st, 1 hdc in next st, 1 sc in next st, 1 sl st in each of next 4 sts, 1 sc in next st, 1 hdc in next st, (1 dc, 1 tr, ch 2, 1 tr, 1 dc) in next st] twice, omit [1 dc, 1 tr, ch 2, 1 tr, 1 dc] on last rep, sl st in third ch of beginning ch 3 (48 sts).

Round 6 (RS): sl st in next st, sl st in 2-ch sp, ch 3, [1 dc, ch 2, 2 dc] in same 2-ch sp, [1 dc in each of next 12 sts, (2 dc, ch 2, 2 dc) in 2-ch sp] four times, omit [2 dc, ch 2, 2 dc] on last rep, sl st in third ch of beginning ch 3 (64 sts).

Round 7 (RS): sl st in next st, sl st in 2-ch sp, ch 3, [1 dc, ch 2, 2 dc] in same 2-ch sp, [1 dc in each of next 16 sts, (2 dc, ch 2, 2 dc) in 2-ch sp] four times, omit [2 dc, ch 2, 2 dc] on last rep, sl st in third ch of beginning ch 3 (80 sts).

Row 8 (RS): sl st in next st, sl st in 2-ch sp, ch 3, [1 dc, ch 2, 2 dc] in same 2-ch sp, [1 dc in each of next 20 sts, (2 dc, ch 2, 2 dc) in 2-ch sp] four times, omit [2 dc, ch 2, 2 dc] on last rep, sl st in third ch of beginning ch 3 (96 sts).

Row 9 (RS): sl st in next st, sl st in 2-ch sp, ch 4 (counts as 1 hdc, ch 2), 1 hdc in same 2-ch sp, [1 hdc in each of next 24 sts, (1 hdc, ch 2, 1 hdc) in 2-ch sp] four times, omit [1 hdc, ch 2, 1 hdc] on last rep, sl st in second ch of beginning ch 4 (104 sts).
Fasten off **yarn B**.

Row 10 (RS): using **yarn A**, in any 2-ch sp, ch 1 (does not count as st), [(1 sc, ch 2, 1 sc) in 2-ch sp, 1 sc in each of next 26 sts] four times, sl st in beginning sc (112 sts).
Fasten off **yarn A**.

Weave in ends and block.

EARS

Ear one: using **yarn A** and US C/2 (3mm) hook, start with a magic ring.

Row 1 (RS): ch 1, 3 sc into ring, turn (3 sts).

Row 2 (WS): ch 1 (does not count as st), 2 sc in next st, [1 sc, ch 1, 1 sc] in next st, 2 sc in next st, turn (6 sts).

Row 3 (RS): ch 1, 1 sc in each of next 3 sts, [1 sc, ch 1, 1 sc] in next st, 1 sc in each of next 3 sts (8 sts).

Fasten off **yarn A**.

Optional step: using a small amount of **yarn C**, embroider inner ear detail. Sew onto square; only attach bottom edge of the ear to make it stand out from base fabric.

Ear two: rep ear one, replacing **yarn A** with **yarn D**.

EYE PATCH

This is worked in a continuous round; do not close or fasten off round until instructed.

Using **yarn E** and US C/2 (3mm) hook, start with a magic ring.

Round 1 (RS): ch 1 (does not count as st throughout), 6 sc into ring (6 sts).

Round 2 (RS): [3 sc in next st, 1 sc in each of next 2 sts] twice (10 sts).

Round 3 (RS): 1 sc in next st, [3 sc in next st, 1 sc in each of next 4 sts] twice, omit 1 sc on last rep, sl st in beginning sc (14 sts).

Fasten off **yarn E**.

Sew onto square.

SPOTS

Spot one: using **yarn D** and US C/2 (3mm) hook, start with a magic ring.

Row 1 (RS): ch 1 (does not count as st throughout), 4 sc into ring, turn (4 sts).

Row 2 (WS): ch 1, 2 sc in each st (8 sts).

Fasten off **yarn D**.

Sew onto square.

Spot two: rep spot one, using **yarn F**.

FINISHING TOUCHES

Embroidery: Using black embroidery thread and a yarn needle, embroider on your cat's nose, mouth, whiskers, and any other details you'd like.

Backstitch is useful for creating outlines and lines. Bring the needle through from the back of the work. From the front and in one motion, take the needle through to the back a short distance along to the right, then draw it through the work to the front the same distance along to the left from the beginning of the stitch. Continue from right to left by inserting the needle through from front to back at the point where the last stitch emerged.

Eyes: If using safety eyes, attach and secure them in place following the manufacturer's instructions. If you are intending to give the square to a child, embroider on the eyes using the same black thread as for the rest of the details.

Sewing crocheted details to a square: Leave a long tail of yarn when fastening off the last row/round of the crochet piece/detail.

Place the piece on top of the square so that the right sides of both are facing you.

Pin in place and sew on the piece using yarn needle and yarn tail with an overcast stitch (see page 124) through either/both loops and into square.

Fasten off the yarn once the piece is completely attached and weave in the end.

NOTES: Use US G/6 (4mm) hook unless otherwise instructed.

Customize your square and make it your own. Change colors, add more/fewer spots, or embroider on details to personalize your cat square.

Safety eyes are a choking hazard. If you intend to use this square for a small child, please embroider on eyes.

Use image of the square as reference to achieve final look.

Classic Patchwork

Use up leftover yarn in this square to create a patchwork look.

Using **yarn A**, start with a magic ring.

Round 1 (RS): ch 3 (counts as 1 dc), 2 dc into ring, ch 2, [3 dc, ch 2 into ring] three times, sl st in third ch of beginning ch 3, fasten off **yarn A** (12 sts).

Round 2 (RS): using **yarn B**, in any 2-ch sp, [ch 3, 2 dc, ch 2, 3 dc] in same 2-ch sp, [(3 dc, ch 2, 3 dc) in next 2-ch sp] three times, sl st in third ch of beginning ch 3, fasten off **yarn B** (24 sts).

Round 3 (RS): using **yarn C**, in any 2-ch sp, [ch 3, 2 dc, ch 2, 3 dc] in same 2-ch sp, [skip next 3 sts, 3 dc in st sp, skip next 3 sts, (3 dc, ch 2, 3 dc) in next 2-ch sp] four times, omit [3 dc, ch 2, 3 dc] on last rep, sl st in third ch of beginning ch 3, fasten off **yarn C** (36 sts).

Round 4 (RS): using **yarn D**, in any 2-ch sp, [ch 3, 2 dc, ch 2, 3 dc] in same 2-ch sp, [skip next 3 sts, (3 dc in st sp, skip next 3 sts) twice, (3 dc, ch 2, 3 dc) in next 2-ch sp] four times, omit [3 dc, ch 2, 3 dc] on last rep, sl st in third ch of beginning ch 3, fasten off **yarn D** (48 sts).

Row 5 (RS): using **yarn E**, in any 2-ch sp,

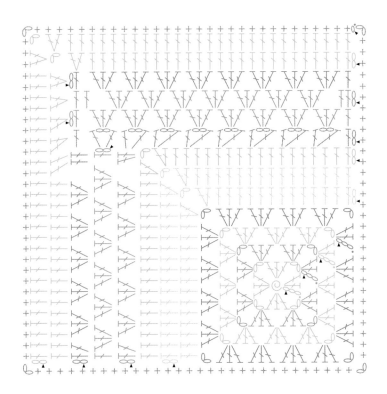

| SKILL LEVEL |

HOOK SIZE	BLOCK SIZE
US E/4 (3.5mm)	6 x 6in (15 x 15cm)

TECHNIQUES

Changing color on row/round (see page 121)
Working into round/row ends (see page 125)

YARN/COLORS

Sample uses Paintbox Cotton DK

A = Buttercup Yellow (#423)
B = Bubblegum Pink (#451)
C = Blush Pink (#454)
D = Marine Blue (#434)
E = Dusty Rose (#442)
F = Washed Teal (#433)
G = Paper White (#401)
H = Lime Green (#429)

STITCHES

ch—chain
sl st—slip stitch
sc—single crochet
dc—double crochet

MIX AND MATCH

Page 30 ＋ Page 82

CHART KEY

For symbol key, see page 122

ch 2 (does not count as st), 1 dc in same sp, 1 dc in each of next 12 sts, [2 dc, ch 2, 2 dc] in 2-ch sp, 1 dc in each of next 12 sts, 1 dc in 2-ch sp, turn (30 sts).

Row 6 (WS): ch 2, 1 dc in each st until next 2-ch sp, [2 dc, ch 2, 2 dc] in 2-ch sp, 1 dc in each st to end, fasten off **yarn E**, turn (34 sts).

Row 7 (RS): rep row 6 using **yarn A**, fasten off **yarn A**, turn (38 sts).

Row 8 (WS): using **yarn B**, ch 2, 2 dc in same st, [skip next 2 sts, 3 dc in next st] five times, skip next 3 sts, 2 dc in 2-ch sp, turn (19 sts).

Row 9 (RS): ch 2, 1 dc in same st, skip next st, [3 dc in st sp, skip next 3 sts] five times, 3 dc in next st sp, skip next st, 1 dc in end st, fasten off **yarn B**, turn (20 sts).

Row 10 (WS): using **yarn F**, ch 2, 1 dc in same st, 1 dc in next st sp, [skip next 3 sts, 3 dc in next st sp] five times, skip next 3 sts, 1 dc in next st sp, 1 dc in end st, fasten off **yarn F**, turn (19 sts).

Row 11 (RS): using **yarn G**, in first st of row 7, ch 2, 1 dc in same st, [skip next 2 sts, (1 dc, ch 2, 1 dc) in next st] six times, skip ch sp, [1 dc, ch 2, 1 dc] in side of each of next 2 dc, 1 dc in end st, fasten off **yarn G**, turn (18 sts).

Row 12 (WS): using **yarn H**, ch 2, 1 dc in same st, 3 dc in each 2-ch sp, 1 dc in end st, turn (26 sts).

Row 13 (RS): ch 2, 1 dc in same st, 1 dc in next st sp, [skip next 3 sts, 3 dc in next st sp] seven times, skip next 3 sts, 1 dc in next st sp, 1 dc in end st, fasten off **yarn H**, turn (25 sts).

Row 14 (WS): using **yarn D**, ch 2, 1 dc in same st, skip next st, [3 dc in st sp, skip next 3 sts] seven times, 3 dc in next st sp, skip next st, 1 dc in end st, fasten off **yarn D**, turn (26 sts).

Row 15 (RS): using **yarn C**, ch 2, 1 dc in same st, 1 dc in each of next 24 sts, 2 dc in next st, ch 2, 2 dc in side of each of next 4 sts, 1 dc in each st to end, fasten off **yarn C**, turn (54 sts).

Row 16 (WS): rep row 6 using **yarn A**, fasten off **yarn A**, turn (58 sts).

BORDER

Round 1 (RS): using **yarn G**, in last st of row 16, ch 1, 1 sc in same st, 1 sc in each of next 28 sts, [1 sc, ch 1, 1 sc] in next 2-ch sp, 1 sc in each of next 29 sts, ch 2, evenly space 29 sc along side, [1 sc, ch 1, 1 sc] in next 2-ch sp, evenly space 29 sc along next side, ch 2, sl st in beginning sc (120 sts).
Fasten off **yarn G**.

Weave in ends and block.

THE PROJECTS

Are you feeling inspired? Use some of the colorful
squares you have been experimenting with to make one
of the four fun projects that follow.

<table>
<tr><td>

SKILL LEVEL

</td></tr>
</table>

HOOK SIZE	WALL HANGING SIZE
US H/8 (5mm)	(excluding fringe) 9½ x 8in (24 x 20cm)

TECHNIQUES

Working into round/row ends
(see page 125)

MATERIALS

1 x 12in (30cm) wooden dowel

Note: As long as it's slightly longer than the width of your crochet piece, any type of thin rod or stick will work.

YARN/COLORS

Sample uses Scheepjes Cahlista

A = Snow White (#106)
B = Ultra Violet (#282)
C = Cyan (#397)
D = Green Yellow (#245)
E = Yellow Gold (#208)
F = Tangerine (#281)
G = Tulip (#222)
H = Shocking Pink (#114)

STITCHES

ch—chain
sc—single crochet

CHART KEY

For symbol key, see page 122

Rainbow Arch Wall Hanging

A larger version of the rainbow arch on page 92,
this wall hanging will add some boho style to your home.
You could make one for all your friends.

Follow the instructions on page 92 to make one Rainbow Arch square. Please note that this project uses a different type of yarn to the original square.

TURNING THE SQUARE INTO A WALL HANGING

Row 1 (RS): using yarn A, in top corner 2-ch sp, ch 1 (does not count as st throughout), 1 sc in 2-ch sp, 1 sc in each of next 30 sts, 1 sc in next 2-ch sp, turn (32 sts).

Row 2 (WS): ch 1, 1 sc in each st across, turn (32 sts).

Row 3 (RS): rep row 2, do not turn (32 sts). Next row/round will be worked around next three sides of work: ch 1, 1 sc in side of sc just made, 1 sc in side of each of next 2 rows, [1 sc in each of next 30 sts, ch 2, skip next 2-ch sp] twice, 1 sc in each of next 30 sts, 1 sc in side of each of next 3 rows, ch 1 (96 sts).

JOINING DOWEL

For the next row, work stitches over dowel and into row to secure together: 1 sc in side of sc just made, 1 sc in each of next 30 sts, 1 sc in side of next sc, ch 48, fasten off yarn A and leave long tail.

Using a yarn needle, sew ch to sc on the other end.

MAKING THE FRINGE

To make one piece of fringe, cut two pieces of yarn each measuring approx. 23½in (60cm). Place them together and fold in half. Insert a crochet hook (any size) horizontally at the bottom of corresponding color and out the other end. Pull both strands of yarn through. Take end of yarn and put through loop that was created by threading yarn through piece and pull tight to secure.

For each leg of rainbow, make one piece of fringe for yarn D, yarn F, yarn G, and yarn H and two pieces of fringe for yarn B, yarn C, and yarn E. Once all 20 pieces of fringe have been attached, trim ends so that fringe is even and level.

HOOK SIZE	PILLOW SIZE
US E/4 (3.5mm)	(excluding fringe)
	15¾ x 15¾in
	(40 x 40cm)

TECHNIQUES
Joining and edging (see pages 124–125)

MATERIALS
1 x 15¾ x 15¾in (40 x 40cm) pillow with cover

YARN/COLORS
Sample uses Scheepjes Softfun

Colorway 1 (make 3):
A = Snow (#2412)
B = Canary (#2518)
C = Rose (#2514)
D = Botanical (#2615)

Colorway 2 (make 3):
A = Snow (#2412)
B = Apple (#2516)
C = Butterscotch (#2610)
D = Orchid (#2657)

Colorway 3 (make 3):
A = Snow (#2412)
B = Cantaloupe (#2652)
C = Hot Pink (#2495)
D = Mint (#2640)

CHART KEY
For symbol key, see page 122

Citrus Slice Pillow

A cute, bright addition to any home, just imagine a whole row of these pillows adorning a living room. This block is a great way to explore color.

———

The pillow is made up of nine squares in three different colorways, which are joined and then hand sewn onto a pre-made pillow cover.

Follow the instructions on page 25 to make the squares. Each square is complete after round 10 for this project.

TURNING THE SQUARES INTO A PILLOW
Using **yarn A** and a yarn needle, sew the squares together using your preferred method. Mattress stitch (see page 124) is used in the pillow pictured. Refer to the image for square arrangement.

Once the squares are joined, using **yarn A**, work a simple edging of single crochet around the entire piece (see page 125). Sew the crochet piece onto the front of the pillow cover using your preferred method. Overcasting (see page 124) is used in the pillow pictured.

HOOK SIZE	BLANKET SIZE
US G/6 (4mm)	36 x 36in (92 x 92cm)

TECHNIQUES

Working with multiple colors at the same time/
intarsia crochet (see page 121)

Changing color on row/round (see page 121)

Slip stitch joining (see below)

YARN/COLORS

Sample uses Paintbox Cotton DK

A = Pillar Red (#415)

B = Kingfisher Blue (#435)

C = Marine Blue (#434)

D = Blood Orange (#420)

E = Lime Green (#429)

F = Buttercup Yellow (#423)

G = Spearmint Green (#426)

STITCHES

slip stitch joining—with right side of blocks
facing up and holding the working yarn at
the back of the blocks, insert hook through
the back loop on one block and through the
corresponding back loop on the second block,
pick up yarn from the back of your work and
make a slip stitch. Continue in this way until
all stitches have been joined.

CHART KEY

For symbol key, see page 122

Rainbow Chevron Blanket

Snuggle up in the colder months with this cozy blanket.
You can easily make it smaller and give it as a new
baby gift, or larger to cover a whole bed.

Using the Two-color Intarsia Square on page
40, make in the following colors:

Six squares using **yarn A** and **yarn B**.

Six squares using **yarn B** and **yarn C**.

Six squares using **yarn C** and **yarn D**.

Six squares using **yarn D** and **yarn E**.

Six squares using **yarn E** and **yarn F**.

Six squares using **yarn F** and **yarn G**.

Using the layout chart, join the squares in
six rows of six squares using the slip stitch
joining method (see panel, left). Match the
joining yarn color to that of the squares
being joined.

HOOK SIZE	BOX SIZE
US C/2 (3mm)	6 x 6 x 6in (15 x 15 x 15cm)

TECHNIQUES
Working with multiple colors at the same time/ intarsia crochet (see page 121)

Changing color on row/round (see page 121)

Slip stitch joining (see below)

YARN/COLORS
Sample uses Scheepjes Softfun

A = Mint (#2640)

B = Snow (#2412)

C = Green Tea (#2639)

D = Soft Lime (#2638)

STITCHES
ch—chain

sl st—slip stitch

sc—single crochet

dc—double crochet

slip stitch joining—with right side of blocks facing up and holding the working yarn at the back of the blocks, insert hook through the back loop on one block and through the corresponding back loop on the second block, pick up yarn from the back of your work and make a slip stitch. Continue in this way until all stitches have been joined.

CHART KEY
For symbol key, see page 122

Minty Tones Storage Box

Store children's toys or books in this handy little box. It's so easy and quick to make, why not make one in all the colors of the rainbow?

———

Using the Picnic Time square on page 12, make five squares.

Join the squares together to form a box using the slip stitch joining method (see panel, left) and yarn B.

Using yarn B, work a round of sc in each stitch around the top of the box.

FLOWER
Using yarn A, ch 5 and join with sl st in first ch made to form a ring.

Round 1: ch 1 (does not count as st throughout), [1 sc into ring, ch 2] eight times, sl st in beginning sc, fasten off yarn A.

Round 2: using yarn D, in 2-ch sp, [[(ch 2, 1 dc) twice, ch 2, 1 sl st) in same 2-ch sp, ch 1, skip next st, 1 sl st in next 2-ch sp] eight times, fasten off yarn D.

Weave in ends and sew flower to box.

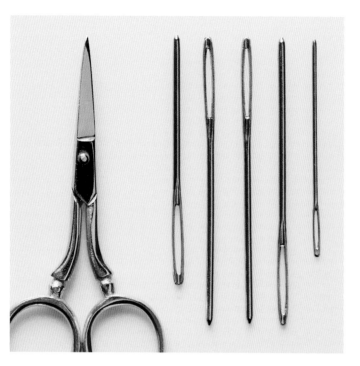

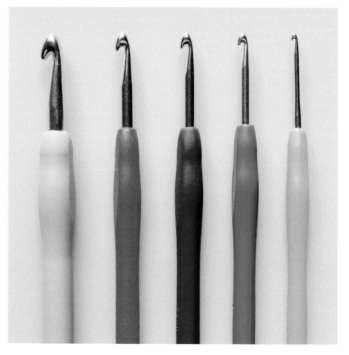

CROCHET BASICS

Do you need to check how to work a popcorn stitch or don't know how to join your squares together? All the techniques you need are explained on the following pages.

Materials and Notions

When you walk into a yarn store, you'll find yourself bombarded with gorgeous yarns in scrumptious colors, differing weights, and all types of textures. The choice is exciting but can be a little perplexing, and the same is true for hooks and accessories. Use this guide to find out what you need to get started.

YARN CHOICE

Suitable yarns for crochet range from very fine cotton to bulky wool. As a general rule, yarns that have a smooth texture and a medium or high twist are the easiest to work with. For making blankets or pillows, a medium-weight yarn is probably best, as it works up quickly, has good drape and stitch definition, and provides warmth. All of the granny squares in this book have been worked in DK/light worsted yarn.

Another thing to consider while standing in front of all that yarn is the fiber content and the kind of drape that you would like to achieve in your project. Before purchasing enough yarn to complete a project, it's a good idea to buy just one ball. Make a test swatch, wash it following the instructions on the ball band, block it to shape, and see whether you are comfortable using the yarn and whether it turns out how you'd intended (see page 123).

YARN FIBERS

Yarns come in a range of different fibers and fiber combinations.

Cotton and cotton mixes

All of the squares in this book are made of cotton and cotton-mix yarns as they come in beautiful colors. This type of yarn can be a little stiff to work with at first, but the stitches are crisp and neat. A cotton mix is usually softer to work with, yet still retains crisp, neat stitch definition. Crocheted pieces made of cotton or a cotton mix are very durable.

Acrylic

Acrylic yarn is a perfect choice for beginners and popular with crochet enthusiasts. It's great for practicing stitches and techniques and testing color combinations. Acrylic yarns come in a huge array of colors and are an affordable choice for your first project. Although acrylic can pill and lose its shape eventually, it does have the benefit of being machine-washable, making it a good choice for items that may require frequent washing.

Wool

Wool is an excellent choice for making blankets or larger crocheted projects. It is a resilient fiber that feels good to crochet with and has great stitch definition. Do find out whether or not the wool can be machine-washed.

Combination yarns

A yarn comprised of both wool and synthetic fiber is a dependable choice. Picking something that has a small percentage of synthetic fiber (for example, nylon or acrylic) makes a nice yarn to work with and launder.

Novelty yarns

Although novelty yarns are tactile and enticing, they are not easy to work with. You can use a splash of novelty yarn to add some interest, but on the whole they are tricky to use and also hide the stitches.

CROCHET HOOKS

Hooks come in different sizes and materials. The material a hook is made from can affect your gauge. To start out, it's best to use aluminum hooks, as they have a pointed head and well-defined throat and work well with most yarns. Bamboo hooks are also pleasing to work with, but can be slippery with some yarns. Plastic hooks can be squeaky with synthetic yarns. You can also purchase hooks with soft-grip or wooden handles, which are great to work with, particularly if crochet becomes an obsession.

What size hook?

You may find that using the hook size recommended for a particular yarn or pattern isn't satisfactory, and your work may be too tight or too loose. Try different hook sizes until you are happy with the completed swatch. Ultimately, you want to use a hook and yarn weight that you are comfortable with—yarn/hook recommendations are not set in stone. Be aware that not all yarn labels give a recommended hook size. Use the recommended knitting needle size as a guide, or a hook one or two sizes bigger.

NOTIONS

Although all you need to get started is a hook and some yarn, it's handy to have the following items in your work bag.

Scissors

Use a pair of small, sharp embroidery scissors.

Ruler and measuring tape

A rigid ruler is best for measuring gauge. A sturdy measuring tape is good for taking larger measurements.

Stitch markers

Split-ring markers are handy for keeping track of the first stitch of a row or round, particularly when starting out. Also use them to hold the working loop when you put your work down for the night.

Pins

Use rustproof, glass-headed pins for wet and steam blocking.

Needles

Yarn or tapestry needles are used for sewing seams and weaving in yarn ends. Choose needles with blunt ends to avoid splitting stitches. Yarn needles have different-sized eyes, so choose one that will accommodate the weight of yarn you will be using.

Starting and Finishing

Crochet can be worked in rows, beginning with a foundation chain, or in rounds, working outward from a foundation ring of chain stitches or a magic ring. See page 118 for a reminder of how to work the basic crochet stitches.

Holding the hook and yarn

The most common way of holding the hook is shown here, but if this doesn't feel comfortable to you, try grasping the flat section of the hook between your thumb and forefinger as if you were holding a knife.

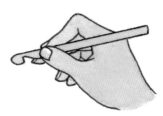

1 Holding the hook like a pen is the most widely used method. Center the tips of your right thumb and forefinger over the flat section of the hook.

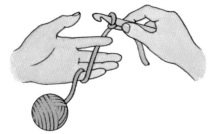

2 To control the supply and keep an even tension on the yarn, loop the short end of the yarn over your left forefinger, and take the yarn coming from the ball loosely around the little finger on the same hand. Use the middle finger on the same hand to help hold the work. If you are left-handed, hold the hook in your left hand and the yarn in your right.

Making a slip knot

1 Loop the yarn as shown, insert the hook into the loop, catch the yarn with the hook, and pull it through to make a loop over the hook.

2 Gently pull the yarn to tighten the loop around the hook and complete the slip knot.

Foundation chain

The pattern will tell you how many chains to make. This may be a specific number or a multiple. If a pattern tells you to make a multiple of 3 + 2, this does not mean make a multiple of 5. It means that you should make a multiple of 3 and then add 2 chains—e.g. 3 + 2, 6 + 2, 9 + 2, and so on. You may also be instructed to add a turning chain for the first row.

1 Holding the hook with the slip knot in your right hand and the yarn in your left hand, wrap the yarn over the hook. Draw the yarn through to make a new loop and complete the first chain stitch.

2 Repeat this process, drawing a new loop of yarn through the loop already on the hook until the foundation chain is the required length. Count each V-shaped loop on the front of the chain as one chain stitch, except for the loop on the hook, which is not counted. If your chain stitches are tight, try using a larger hook for the foundation chain. After every few stitches, move up the thumb and finger that are grasping the chain to keep the chain stitches even.

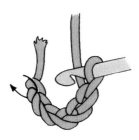

Foundation ring

1 Work a short length of foundation chain as specified in the pattern. Join the chains into a ring by working a slip stitch into the first chain of the foundation chain.

2 Work the first round of stitches into the center of the ring unless specified otherwise. At the end of the round, the final stitch is usually joined to the first stitch with a slip stitch.

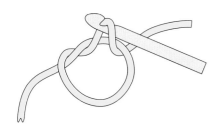

Magic ring

Use this alternative to a foundation ring for working in the round when you want to prevent a hole in the center of your work. Wrap the yarn into a ring, insert the hook, and draw a loop through. Work the first round of crochet stitches into this ring, then pull the yarn tail tightly to close the ring.

Turning and starting chains

When working crochet, you will need to work a specific number of extra chains at the beginning of each row or round. When the work is turned at the end of a straight row, the extra chains are called a turning chain, and when they are worked at the beginning of a round, they are called a starting chain.

The extra chains bring the hook up to the correct height for the stitch you will be working next. The turning or starting chain is counted as the first stitch of the row or round, except when working single crochet where the single turning chain is ignored. A chain may be longer than the number required for the stitch, and in that case counts as one stitch plus a number of chains.

At the end of the row, the final stitch is usually worked into the turning chain at the beginning of the previous row. The final stitch may be worked into the top chain of the turning chain or into another specified stitch of the chain. At the end of a round, the final stitch is usually joined to the starting chain with a slip stitch.

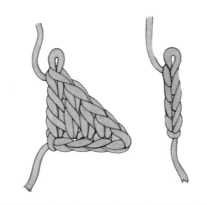

NUMBER OF TURNING CHAINS

Single crochet (sc): 1 turning chain

Half double crochet (hdc): 2 turning chains

Double crochet (dc): 3 turning chains

Treble crochet (tr): 4 turning chains

Double treble crochet (dtr): 5 turning chains

Triple treble crochet (trtr): 6 turning chains

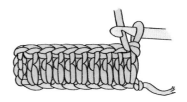

Fastening off

When you have completed your crochet, cut the yarn about 6in (15cm) from the last stitch. Wrap the yarn over the hook and draw the yarn end through the loop on the hook. Gently pull the yarn to tighten the last stitch, then weave in the yarn end.

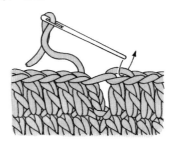

Finishing the last round

For a neater finish, don't use a slip stitch to join the last stitch of the final round to the first stitch of the round. Instead, fasten off the yarn after the last stitch, thread a yarn needle with the end of yarn, and pass it under the top loops of the first stitch of the round and back through the center of the last stitch.

Weaving in ends

At the end of making your project, you will need to weave in any yarn ends from changing colors and sewing seams. For crochet worked in rows, use a yarn needle to sew in ends diagonally on the wrong side. For crochet worked in rounds, sew in ends under stitches for a couple of inches. If the pattern doesn't allow this, sew under a few stitches, then up through the back of a stitch, and under a few more stitches on the next row.

Basic Stitches

All crochet stitches are based on a loop pulled through another loop by a hook.
There are only a few stitches to master, each of a different length. Here is a concise guide
to the basic stitches used to make the granny squares.

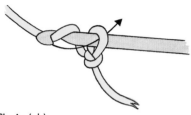

Chain (ch)
Wrap the yarn over the hook and pull it through the loop on the hook to form a new loop on the hook.

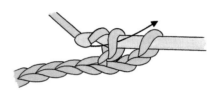

Extended single crochet (ext sc)
Insert the hook into the specified stitch, yarn over hook, and pull it through the stitch (2 loops on hook). Chain 1. Yarn over hook and pull it through both loops.

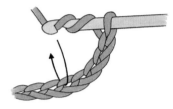

Treble crochet (tr)
Yarn over hook twice, insert the hook into the specified stitch, yarn over hook, and pull it through the stitch (4 loops on hook). *Yarn over hook and pull it through two loops; repeat from * twice more.

Slip stitch (sl st)
Insert the hook into the specified stitch, wrap the yarn over the hook, and pull it through the stitch and the loop on the hook.

Half double crochet (hdc)
Yarn over hook, insert the hook into the specified stitch, yarn over hook, and pull it through the stitch (3 loops on hook). Yarn over hook and pull it through all three loops.

Single crochet (sc)
Insert the hook into the specified stitch, wrap the yarn over the hook, and pull it through the stitch (2 loops on hook). Yarn over hook and pull it through both loops.

Double crochet (dc)
Yarn over hook, insert the hook into the specified stitch, yarn over hook, and pull it through the stitch (3 loops on hook). *Yarn over hook and pull it through two loops; repeat from * once more.

MAKING TALLER STITCHES
You can make taller stitches by wrapping the yarn over the hook as many times as you wish before inserting the hook into the specified stitch. For example, wrap the yarn over the hook three times to make a double treble crochet (dtr). Make four wraps for a triple treble crochet (trtr) and so on. Complete the stitch in the same way as treble crochet, working off two loops at a time in the usual way.

Simple Stitch Variations

Basic stitches can be varied in many ways to achieve different effects. These simple variations are all made by inserting the hook in different places in the crochet to work the stitches.

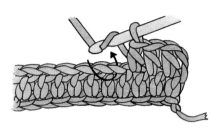

Through the front loop (fl)

Rather than inserting the hook under both top loops to work the next stitch in the usual way, insert it only under the front loop.

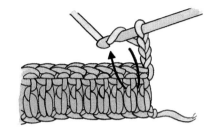

Around the front post (fp)

Work around the stem of the stitch, inserting the hook from front to back, around the post, and to the front again.

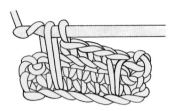

Into a row below (spike stitch)

Spike stitches are made by inserting the hook one or more rows below the previous row. To work a single crochet spike stitch, for example, insert the hook as directed by the pattern, wrap the yarn over the hook and draw it through, lengthen the loop to the height of the working row, then complete the stitch.

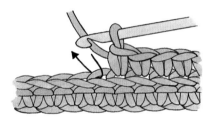

Through the back loop (bl)

Rather than inserting the hook under both top loops to work the next stitch in the usual way, insert it only under the back loop.

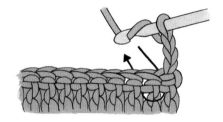

Around the back post (bp)

Work around the stem of the stitch, inserting the hook from back to front, around the post, and to the back again.

Into a chain space (ch sp)

Insert the hook into the space below a chain or chains. Here, a tr is being worked into a ch sp.

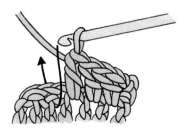

Into a stitch space (st sp)

Insert the hook between the stitches of the previous row, instead of into a stitch itself.

Special Stitches

By working multiple stitches in the same place or working several stitches together at the top, or a combination of both, you can create interesting shapes, patterns, and textures. The turning or starting chain may be counted as the first stitch of a cluster, bobble, popcorn, or puff stitch.

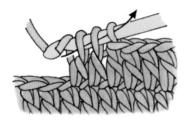

Decrease (e.g. sc2tog, dc3tog)

One or two stitches can be decreased by working two or three incomplete stitches together. Work the specified number of stitches, omitting the final stage (the last yarn over) of each stitch so that the last loop of each stitch remains on the hook. Wrap the yarn over the hook and draw it through all of the loops on the hook. The method is the same for all the basic crochet stitches.

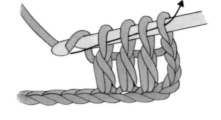

Cluster (cl)

A cluster can be made from a multiple of any of the basic crochet stitches. Work the specified number of stitches in the places indicated in the pattern, omitting the final stage of each stitch so that the last loop of each stitch remains on the hook. Wrap the yarn over the hook and draw it through all of the loops on the hook.

Popcorn (pc)

A popcorn is a group of double crochet or longer stitches worked in the same place, and then folded and closed at the top so that the popcorn is raised from the background stitches. Work the specified number of stitches in the same place. Take the hook out of the working loop and insert it under both top loops of the first stitch of the popcorn. Pick up the working loop with the hook and draw it through to fold the group of stitches and close the popcorn at the top. Chain 1 to secure.

Increase (e.g. 5 dc in next ch)

This technique is used to increase the total number of stitches when shaping an item, or to create a decorative effect such as a shell. Simply work the required number of stitches in the same place. Increases may be worked at the edges of flat pieces, or at any point along a row or round.

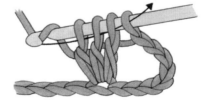

Bobble (bo)

A bobble is a group of between three and six double crochet or longer stitches worked in the same place and closed at the top. Work the specified number of stitches, omitting the final stage of each stitch so that the last loop of each stitch remains on the hook. Wrap the yarn over the hook and draw it through all of the loops on the hook.

Puff stitch (ps)

A puff stitch is a group of half double crochet stitches worked in the same place. Work the specified number of stitches, omitting the final stage of each stitch so that two loops of each stitch remain on the hook. Wrap the yarn over the hook and draw it through all of the loops on the hook.

Colorwork

Most of the granny square patterns use a single color for each row or round, with the new color being joined at the end of a row or round. Tapestry and intarsia designs involve using multiple colors across the row. In tapestry crochet, the unworked color is carried behind the row and woven in. Intarsia crochet features large and sometimes irregularly shaped sections of different colors, and each section is worked with a separate ball of yarn.

Changing color on a row

When working the last stitch of the old color, omit the final stage (the last yarn over) to leave the stitch incomplete. Wrap the new yarn over the hook and draw it through all of the loops on the hook to complete the stitch. The new yarn will form the top loops of the next stitch in the new color.

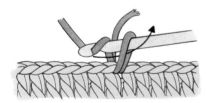

Changing color on a round

Method 1: When joining the last stitch of the round to the first stitch using a slip stitch, work the joining slip stitch using the new color.
Method 2 (above): Insert the hook where required and draw up a loop of the new color, leaving a 4in (10cm) tail. Work the specified number of starting chains. Continue with the new yarn.

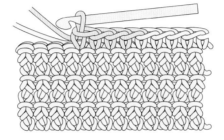

Tapestry crochet

1 Change to the new color (pink) in the usual way. Continue following the pattern, carrying the unused yarn (blue) along the top of the previous row at the back of the work and crocheting over it. After the next color change, continue to carry and work over the unused yarn in the same way.

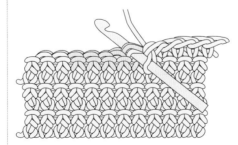

2 On the next and all other rows, insert the hook under the carried yarn and into the stitch to lock the carried yarn in place.

Intarsia crochet

Use a separate ball or bobbin of yarn for each area of color. If the same color is used twice across the row, you will need two separate balls of it.

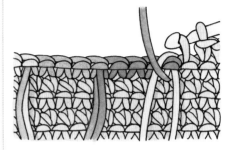

1 Follow the pattern, changing colors where indicated in the usual way and dropping the unused yarns to the wrong side of the work. At each color change on subsequent rows, make sure that you loop the new yarn around the old one on the wrong side of the work to prevent holes.

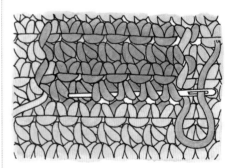

2 Take extra care when dealing with all the yarn ends on a piece of intarsia. Carefully weave each end into an area of crochet worked in the same color so that it will not be visible on the right side.

Reading Patterns and Charts

With all those symbols, abbreviations, and charts, crochet can seem daunting and complex to begin with. A little explanation, though, and all becomes clear.

Abbreviations are used to make crochet patterns quicker and easier to follow. Abbreviations and chart symbols may vary from one pattern publisher to another, so always check that you understand the system in use before commencing work. Some patterns use special abbreviations and symbols and specific stitch instructions, and these are explained with each pattern.

UNDERSTANDING SYMBOLS

SYMBOL	MEANING
*	Start of repeat
**	End of last repeat
[ ]	Repeat the instructions within the brackets the stated number of times in the specified place
( )	Can either be explanatory (counts as 1 dc) or can be read as a group of stitches worked in the same place (1 dc, ch 2, 1 dc)
▶	An arrowhead indicates the beginning of a row or round

SYMBOLS JOINED AT TOP

A group of symbols joined at the top should be worked together at the top, as in cluster stitches and for decreasing (e.g. sc2tog, dc3tog)

SYMBOLS JOINED AT BASE

Symbols joined at the base should all be worked into the same stitch or space below

SYMBOLS JOINED AT TOP AND BASE

Sometimes a group of stitches are joined at both top and bottom, making a puff, bobble, or popcorn

SYMBOLS ON A CURVE

Sometimes symbols are drawn at an angle, depending on the construction of the stitch pattern

DISTORTED SYMBOLS

Some symbols may be lengthened, curved, or spiked, to indicate where the hook is inserted below

SYMBOLS AND ABBREVIATIONS

SYMBOL	MEANING	ABBREVIATION
○	Chain	ch
•	Slip stitch	sl st
+	Single crochet	sc
T	Half double crochet	hdc
‡	Double crochet	dc
‡	Treble crochet	tr
‡	Double treble crochet	dtr
‡	Triple treble crochet	trtr
(e.g. cluster of 3 dc)	Cluster	cl
(e.g. bobble of 5 dc)	Bobble	bo
(e.g. puff of 5 hdc)	Puff stitch	ps
(e.g. popcorn of 5 dc)	Popcorn	pc
(e.g. sc through back loop)	Back loop	bl
(e.g. hdc through front loop)	Front loop	fl
(	Back post	bp
)	Front post	fp
—	Beginning	beg
—	Chain space	ch sp
—	Repeat	rep
—	Right side / Wrong side	RS / WS
—	Stitch (es)	st (s)
—	Together	tog
—	Yarn over	yo

READING CHARTS

Each design in this book is accompanied by a chart, which should be read together with the written instructions. Once you are used to the symbols, they are quick and easy to follow. All charts are read from the right side.

Charts in rows

- Right-side rows start at the right, and are read from right to left.
- Wrong-side rows start at the left, and are read from left to right.
- The beginning of each row is indicated by an arrow.

Charts in rounds

These charts begin at the center, and each round is read counterclockwise when working with the RS facing, or clockwise when working with the WS facing. The beginning of each round is indicated by an arrow.

CALCULATING YARN AMOUNTS

When planning a large project using granny squares, the best way to calculate how much yarn you will need is to make a few squares in the yarn and color combination you intend to use, then unravel them. Measure the amount of yarn used for each color, take the average length, and multiply by the number of squares you intend to make. Add extra yarn for joining squares and working edgings.

Gauge and Blocking

It's important to crochet a test swatch before you start your project to establish gauge. To finish off your square neatly, you will need to block it. You can use the gauge swatch to test blocking and cleaning methods.

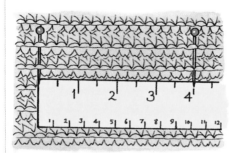

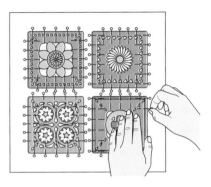

MEASURING GAUGE

No two people will crochet to the exact same gauge, even when working with identical yarn and hooks. Always make a test swatch before starting a project so that you can compare your gauge with the pattern gauge and get an idea of how the finished project will feel and drape. It's also useful for testing out different color combinations.

To test your gauge, make a sample swatch in the yarn you intend to use following the pattern directions. Block the sample and then measure again. If your swatch is larger, try making another using a smaller hook. If your swatch is smaller, try making another using a bigger hook. Also do this if the fabric feels too loose and floppy or too dense and rigid. Keep trying until you find a hook size that will give you the required gauge, or until you are happy with the drape and feel of your work. Ultimately, it's more important that you use a hook and yarn you are comfortable with than that you rigidly follow the pattern instructions.

BLOCKING

Blocking is crucial to set the stitches and even out the piece. Choose a method based on the care label of the yarn. When in doubt, use the wet method. Use an ironing board or old quilt, or make a blocking board by securing one or two layers of quilter's batting, covered with a sheet of cotton fabric, over a flat board.

Wet method—acrylic and wool/acrylic mix
Using rustproof pins, pin the crochet fabric to the correct measurements on a flat surface and dampen using a spray bottle of cold water. Pat the fabric to help the moisture penetrate. Ease stitches into position, keeping rows and stitches straight. Allow to dry before removing the pins.

Steam method—wools and cottons
Pin out the fabric as above. For fabric with raised stitches, pin it right side up to avoid squashing the stitches; otherwise, pin it wrong side up. Steam lightly, holding the iron 1in (2.5cm) above the fabric. Allow the steam to penetrate for several seconds. It is safer to avoid pressing, but if you choose to do so, cover with a clean towel or cloth first.

Joining and Edging

When making a large project from granny squares, you will need to sew or crochet the squares together before adding an edging. A crochet edging does not just finish off a project with style, but it also helps it to hold its shape and keeps the edges from stretching.

JOINING GRANNY SQUARES

Granny squares can be joined by sewing or by crochet. Pin seams together to help match up the squares and give a neat finish. Use the same yarn that you used for the squares, or a finer yarn, preferably with the same fiber content.

Overcasting

Using a yarn needle, sew through the back or front loops of corresponding stitches. For extra strength, work two stitches into the end loops.

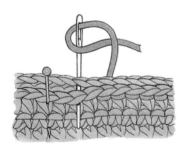

Backstitch

Hold the squares with right sides together. Using a yarn needle, work a line of backstitches along the edge.

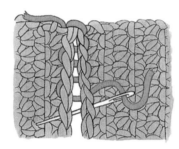

Mattress stitch

Lay the squares wrong side up and with edges touching. Using a yarn needle, weave back and forth around the centers of the stitches, without pulling the stitches too tight.

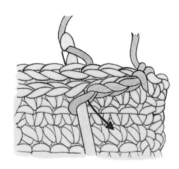

Crochet seams

Join the squares with wrong sides together for a visible seam, or with right sides together for an invisible one. Work a row of slip stitch (above) or single crochet through both top loops of each square. When using this method along the side edges of squares worked in rows, work enough evenly spaced stitches so that the seam is not too tight.

CROCHET-ON EDGINGS

Calculate how many stitches your chosen edging pattern needs, including corners. Start by working a simple edging of single crochet as a base round (see page 125), increasing or decreasing the number of stitches along each edge of the project to match the main edging pattern you have chosen. Make sure increase or decrease stitches are evenly spaced to avoid puckering. Using markers to indicate where pattern repeats will lie will help you to visualize it.

Crochet-on edging calculations

Start the main edging pattern in the corner stitch of the base round. Some designs require a specific multiple of stitches in order to work the pattern repeat. This is written in pattern instructions as:

- Multiple: x + x + 4 corner sts

The corner stitches will be the second single crochet of each corner of the base round, so after working your base round you will have four corner stitches (1 st at each corner). If the pattern requires a multiple of 3 + 2 + 4 corner stitches, you should have a multiple of 3 stitches with 2 stitches remaining along each edge (e.g. 3 + 2, 6 + 2, 9 + 2, and so on), plus 4 corner stitches. Count the stitches along each edge between the corner stitches to check you have the correct number. If you do not, you can work another base round, decreasing or adding stitches evenly as needed.

ATTACHING SEWN-ON EDGINGS

Don't fasten off the yarn in case you need to make adjustments to the length of the edging. Hold the working loop of the edging with a marker to keep it from unraveling. Place the edge of the project and the edge of the edging so that the right sides of both are facing you, with the edging on top. Pin in place and sew on the edging using overcast stitch through the front loops. Make any adjustments to the length of the edging, then fasten off the yarn and use the tail to join the two ends of the border together.

SIMPLE EDGING

Working a simple round of single crochet stitches helps to even out untidy edges at row ends and any uneven stitches. Make the simple edging by crocheting one round of single crochet around the project, working three stitches in each corner. This simple edging provides a good base for a more decorative edging pattern (see page 124).

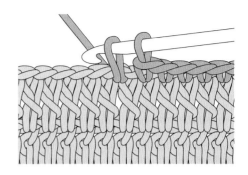

Across the top or bottom edge

When working across the top of a row, work 1 sc into each stitch as you would if working another row. When working across the bottom edge of chain stitches, work 1 sc in the remaining loop of each foundation chain.

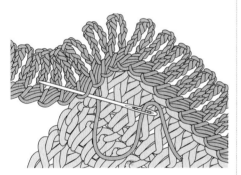

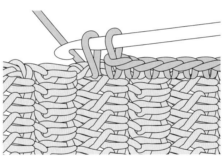

Along sides of row ends

When working on the side edge of a square worked in rows, insert the hook under two threads of the first (or last) stitch of each row. Place the stitches an even distance apart along the edge. Try a short length to test the number of stitches required for a flat result. As a guide:

- **Rows of sc:** 1 sc in side edge of each row.
- **Rows of hdc:** 3 sc in side edge of every two rows.
- **Rows of dc:** 2 sc in side edge of each row.
- **Rows of tr:** 3 sc in side edge of each row.

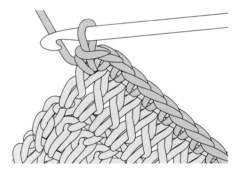

Around corners

You will need to add a couple of stitches at each corner to allow the edging to turn the corner without distorting the shape of the crocheted item. As a guide, corners are normally turned by working 3 sc (or 1 sc, 1 hdc, 1 sc) into the corner. If you find the edging is too wavy or too taut after it has been completed, it will probably get worse once any additional edging has been worked. Take time at this point to pull out this base round and redo it using fewer stitches if the edge is too wavy, or using more stitches if the edge is too taut.

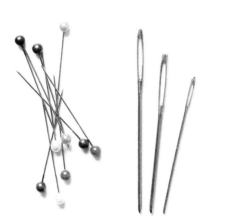

Index

A
acid brights flower 64–5
acrylic yarn 114
around the back post 119
around the front post 119

B backstitch 124
blanket, rainbow chevron 108–9
blocking 123
bobble 120
bobble beads 76–7
bright shimmer 28–9
Brighton rock 72–3

C
chain stitch 118
chains, turning and starting 117
charts, reading 122–3
citrus slice 25–7
    citrus slice pillow 106–7
classic patchwork 99–101
cluster 120
colorblock double crochet
    square 42–3
colorwork 121
    changing color on a round 121
    changing color on a row 121
combination yarns 114
cool-toned triangle 78–9
corners, simple edging around
    125
cotton mix yarns 114
cotton yarn 114
crochet basics 112–25
crochet hooks 115

holding 116
    what size to use 115
crochet seams 124
crocheted flower net 84–5
cross, ombré 66–7
cute kitten 96–8

D
dazzling octagon 80–1
decrease 120
diamond daze 53–5
double crochet 118
double crochet square 30–1

E
edging
    attaching sewn-on edging 125
    crochet-on edging 124
    simple edging 125
extended single crochet 118

F
fastening off 117
finishing 117
flowers
    acid brights flower 64–5
    crocheted flower net 84–5
    four-leaf flower 74–5
    modern floral 34–5
    pop flowers 82–3
    60s floral motif 44–5
    sugar flower 17–19
foundation chain 116
foundation ring 117
four-leaf flower 74–5

G
gauge 123
granny square patterns 10–101
    acid brights flower 64–5
    bobble beads 76–7
    bright shimmer 28–9
    Brighton rock 72–3
    citrus slice 25–7
    classic patchwork 99–101
    colorblock double crochet
    square 42–3
    cool-toned triangle 78–9
    crocheted flower net 84–5
    cute kitten 96–8
    dazzling octagon 80–1
    diamond daze 53–5
    double crochet square 30–1
    four-leaf flower 74–5
    houndstooth pattern 46–7
    intarsia triangles 32–3
    jell-o and ice cream 60–1
    loop and twist 86–8
    modern floral 34–5
    multicolored target 62–3
    ombré cross 66–7
    pastel grid 22–4
    peaches and cream 48–9
    picnic time 12–13
    pop flowers 82–3
    rainbow arch 92–3
    rainbow popcorn 14–16
    rainbow relief 56–7
    scattered hearts 36–7
    single-color granny square
    38–9

60s floral motif 44–5
    sorbet square 50–2
    stripe color block 94–5
    sugar flower 17–19
    sun and clouds 58–9
    technicolor square 70–1
    3D heart 20–1
    two-color intarsia square
    40–1
    warm tones 68–9
    watermelon slice 89–91

H
half double crochet 118
hearts
    scattered hearts 36–7
    3D heart 20–1
houndstooth pattern 46–7

I
increase 120
intarsia
    intarsia crochet 121
    intarsia triangles 32–3
    two-color intarsia square
    40–1
into a chain space 119
into a row below 119
into a stitch space 119

J
jell-o and ice cream 60–1
joining granny squares 124